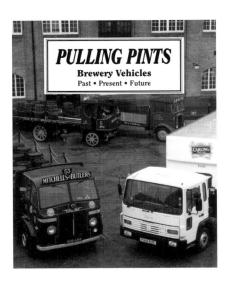

PULLING PINTS

Brewery Vehicles

Past • Present • Future

PULLING PINTS
Brewery Vehicles
Past • Present • Future

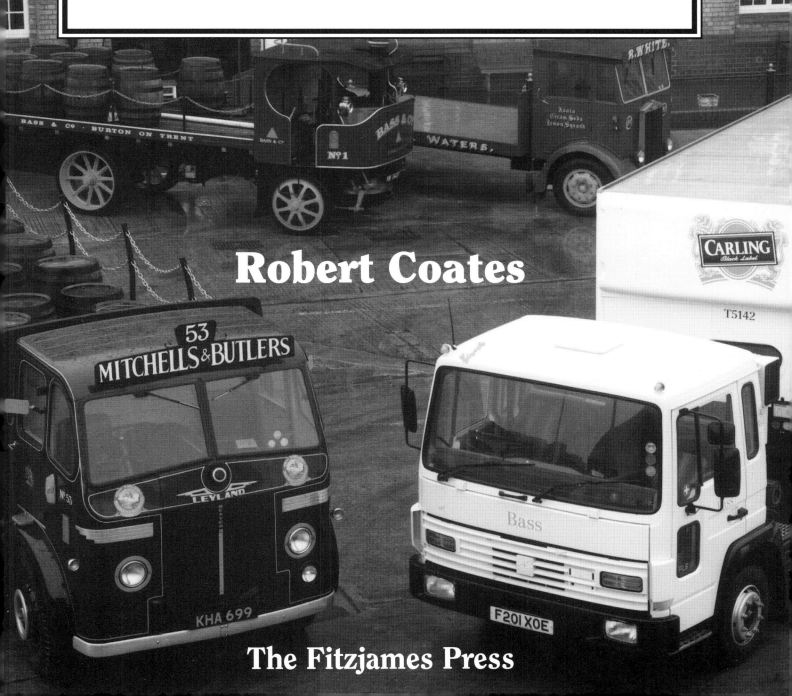

Robert Coates

The Fitzjames Press

THE FITZJAMES PRESS
an imprint of
MOTOR RACING PUBLICATIONS LTD
Unit 6, The Pilton Estate, 46 Pitlake, Croydon CR0 3RY, England

First published 1993

British Library Cataloguing in Publication Data

Coates, Robert
  Pulling Pints
  I. Title
  663.3

ISBN 0-948358-04-1

Typesetting and origination by
Ryburn Publishing Services, Keele University, Staffordshire

Printed in Great Britain by
The Amadeus Press Ltd, Huddersfield, West Yorkshire

Front cover and title page: An impressive array of old and not so old vehicles drawn up in the yard of the 18th century Bass Brewery Museum at Burton on Trent. The Super Sentinel DG4 Steamer dates from 1916 and is regularly 'steamed'. The Albion 7-tonner is in the R. Whites livery of the time and the 1949 Leyland Beaver is beautifully restored to its original Mitchells and Butlers' colours. The modern Volvo FL6-11 artic tractor dates from 1989 and is drawing a 7.6m trailer of 10 tonnes capacity. The outfit is known as the 'urban artic', of which Bass Brewers operate over 600. The Carling Black Label livery was an award winner in the 1992 Commercial Motor annual competition.

Contents

Preface

This collection of brewery vehicle photographs was started many years ago whilst I was working for Whitbread's brewery. As manager responsible for transport I naturally had a long-standing technical interest in vehicles and already possessed a substantial and varied collection of vehicle photographs.

Many people have added to the collection since, and I am ashamed to admit, now that the updated collection is to be collated into book form, that I cannot remember from where all the photos came. Undoubtedly, as the reader will see, the majority are of Whitbread vehicles and some of these came my way by an extraordinary twist of fate.

In the early Eighties a fire at Whitbread's Chiswell Street, London Head Office destroyed parts of the production, distribution and transport offices. On the Saturday following the fire, whilst sorting out its aftermath, I noticed two or three boxes of photographs amongst the rubbish in a refuse skip. Many were badly charred, but they were carefully salvaged and the survivors were added to my own collection – part of which already consisted of duplicates from the same source. I have often thought that if I had not been there or if I had arrived a few minutes later they could well have been lost for all time.

After leaving the brewery I found time to sort the wheat from the chaff with the intention of putting them into a book. Some of the duplicates – where several copies existed of the same photo – were returned to Whitbread's archive, and others were exchanged with the National Motor Museum collection at Beaulieu.

In addition to the above-mentioned sources I should also like to acknowledge the following with grateful thanks for the loan or gift of photos: the breweries of Allied, Bass, Courage, Fremlins, Wethered and Young's; Leyland Motors, Boalloy, Ford Motor Company, MAN UK, Fred Morris, Mrs Thelma Durran and the late Gordon Goddard, former Whitbread Fleet Engineer.

Finally, thanks must particularly be extended to those people who provided the encouragement to complete the book and for the technical advice and guidance. Especial thanks are due to my dear wife whose patience over the 10 years(!) which it has taken me to put this together would have put the saints to shame. Special thanks are also due to Andrew Davis, formerly Fleet Engineer at Whitbread, and latterly a good friend and Fleet Engineer of the Bass Group, who in addition to providing photos, has also given the technical content the 'once-over'. Any remaining technical errors I must take responsibility for myself, but it is comforting to have had such an experienced and expert eye cast over the drafts.

The real purpose behind this book is to share some of these magical old photographs with a wider circle of enthusiasts and friends, at the same time as recording briefly why brewery transport has always been not only so diverse and fascinating but usually at the forefront of technical development.

Ockley, Surrey
May 1993

ROBERT COATES

Introduction

Water is a heavy commodity which, until recent years, usually only required distribution by pipeline – which is a cheap and very effective method. Yet water, mixed with certain other ingredients, can take on a much higher value and require rather different methods of distribution. If the 'certain other ingredients' happen to be malted barley, hops and yeast, the resulting product is very much more valuable and requires extremely precise distribution, especially as it attracts the attention of Her Majesty's Customs and Excise!

So the brewers and distributors of beer – which is really only water mixed with these 'certain other ingredients' – have, from the earliest days of its commercial production, sought ways to distribute it cheaply and effectively without loss of quality. Beer, of course, was also transported before it was produced commercially, when it was still largely a 'home-brew' product, but quantities were small, technology was a thing of the future and, as the distribution element was not conducted along commercial lines, there was little or no incentive to find better or cheaper ways to do it.

The fact that beer is such a heavy product, relative to its value, has always meant that brewers have needed to be in the forefront of vehicle development for heavier – and hence, usually, more productive – transport. Distributors of other heavy products like coal, cement, bricks and flour have faced similar problems and, in some cases, have adopted similar solutions whilst, in other particulars, they have chosen quite different ways. Manufacturers and distributors of soft drinks – another water-based product group which now includes bottled water itself – came onto the commercial scene much later so have, where appropriate, borrowed their technology from the more traditional trades, especially the brewers.

Amongst these heavy-goods trades, brewers have probably enjoyed – at least in the past – a higher profit margin than the others and, wisely, spent some of this money developing not only better methods of brewing and bottling, but also better and safer ways of distributing their product. Amongst today's 'Big Six' brewers, the tradition of suiting the vehicle to the task and of spending time and money on achieving this compatibility has been maintained. Even the accountants can see that its cost-effectiveness is proven time out of hand!

This book, then, is concerned with the development of the brewers' dray in a quest for transport productivity from its earliest beginnings to the present day. In so doing, it traces the history of transporting heavy goods from the viewpoint of the vehicle operator at the same time as being an affectionate look at the vehicles used by what is a very charismatic industry. It is for the reader to judge whether the brewers have, indeed, succeeded in being at the forefront of transport development.

R C

CHAPTER ONE

The Early Days – Horse-Drawn Vehicles

It is a fact which is sometimes overlooked, but the obvious place to start with a history of vehicles is with the horse-drawn variety. Not only are they a source of great interest in themselves but they give many indications of how various components on present day vehicles were originally conceived. Apart from relatively minor improvements, the basic designs for horse-drawn vehicles changed little over a fairly long period of time. Essentially there were three main types: the long-haul waggon*, drawn by as many as nine horses; the local waggon or cart for parcels traffic – of which there was relatively little until around 1800 because communications in general were so poor and communities were far more self-sufficient; and the farmers' waggons, wains and carts. There were, though, as many differences between these types as there were similarities and the whole subject requires detailed study if one is to become at all expert. (*The word waggon is sometimes spelt as wagon, but since there appears to be no particular derivation for either, apart from its root in the Norse word *vagn*, whichever is used seems to be a matter of preference. The writer prefers waggon! *Vagn* may also have developed, via other languages, to give the word 'van' although the more usual derivation for this is from the Middle East as a shortened version of 'caravan'.)

Before the Industrial Revolution, households mainly looked after their own alcoholic needs, brewing their beer, mead and country wines where they were consumed – on the premises. With this cottage-based – or sometimes village-based – economy there was little need for distribution and, indeed, very little to distribute since it was not only beer in which families were self-sufficient.

Just about the only local transport to be seen in those days would have been that of the local carter, conveying parcels traffic between villages or, once the canals and railways became established, from clearing houses to retail outlets. One might also see the local tinker's transport – a pony-trap if he was lucky, but more usually Shanks' pony. Waggons and wains, built to regional patterns and used for bringing in the harvest and for fulfilling other general short-haul transport needs, would also have been commonplace.

However, with the onset of the Industrial Revolution, workers began to forsake the land; trickles at first but swelling to droves of migrants moving into the towns, which quickly became quite densely populated as word of mouth passed on news about higher wages and what they saw as better living and working conditions. Heavy industries such as coal-mining started to grow rapidly and, later, steel and engineering, too, gave rise to the need for consumer-based support industries. One of these support industries was brewing, which began to cater for larger markets, dispersed over wider areas – albeit still quite local by modern standards – and it is from the middle of the 18th century that many of today's brewery companies originate.

But, even before the big breweries were established, there had been a need to carry beer from one place to another over short distances. The very first method, recorded from before the 16th century, consisted of a short pole, or yoke, from which hung four chains, each terminating in a hook. Two hooks were inserted under the rim at each end of a barrel, thus enabling two men to carry it over a short distance. An aquatint, dated 1805, illustrating the use of the two-man yoke, is mentioned in *Whitbread's Brewery* published by Holden & Co. Then, as now, the preferred method of moving casks over very short distances was, of course, to roll it – and this only required one man!

At this stage it is worth pointing out that in the brewing trade the word 'barrel' has a specific meaning as a unit of measure, rather than its colloquial and current usage which describes a wooden cask. The barrel is the key measure around which all the fluid measures in common use are based (see Appendix 1). Even today, when the official measures are litres and hectolitres, the commonly used unit

The earliest of the wheeled drays were simple affairs, with their derivation from the A-frame sled, or barrow, clearly discernible. This fine part-restoration, part-replica is from the Whitbread collection and is only used now for display and publicity purposes. It goes without saying that, in use, the barrels would not have been highly polished with painted tops. Much of the other detail, though, is highly authentic. Note particularly the very wide tyres, designed to spread the load on poor or almost non-existent road surfaces. On some bridges and roads, tolls at one time were actually based on tyre width, recognizing – even in the 18th century – that a more evenly spread load did less damage to a hard surface. Very narrow tyres came into their own in thick mud which, had these 6in tyres sunk in, would have been almost impossible to extricate. Narrow tyres tended to cut through the mud on to firmer surfaces beneath and also presented less resistance as the wheel turned away from the road surface.

A common working dray before the advent of pneumatic tyres. This vehicle was probably built in the East End of London by Bonallack, who later went on to become a major force in vehicle body and trailer building. The shoe-brake is clearly visible and the degree to which the driving seat was raised above the payload is also evident, this being about the only feature which distinguishes it from a normal cart. The lower part of this fitment, on which the men's feet would have rested, was called a 'dash-board' – a term which has come into modern day parlance even though it now relates to a slightly different part.

Six men and a dog delivering to the Stonehenge Inn in 1891. The dray, which lacks any special fittings, appears to be a farm waggon conversion, so is not particularly typical of the period. The work attire of the draymen is of interest; note the heavy boots and the billycock or 'sugarloaf' hats they are wearing, the driver second from right and his 'trouncer' lounging against the shafts (centre).
The more usual configuration for two-horse drays is side-by-side, usually as a well-matched pair. The shafts in this photograph suggest that this is a one-horse waggon, which might normally have been used for the delivery of the lighter-weight bottled beer. The additional horse may well have been provided as a 'cock-horse'. Cock-horses were stabled at the foot of steep hills and were hired out to provide additional pulling power, hence so many 'Cock' Inns, and the reference to a cock-horse to Banbury Cross in the nursery rhyme. Cock-horses were also sometimes known as 'steamers' for obvious reasons and this, too, has given rise to numerous pubs of such a name.

is the barrel. The word 'puncheon', sometimes used in this context, has no specific liquid measure associated with it – it is simply a word for a large cask.

The yoke, however, was inadequate for the larger sizes of cask. So the first real productivity improvement probably occurred in the 16th century when manpower at least partially gave way to animal power with a system employing one man and a horse. The horse drew an A-frame sled upon which, perhaps, two barrels, or even a hogshead or a butt could be drawn. We can see here several 'firsts': the first productivity improvement – payload up from 36 to as much as 108 gallons; the first headcount reductions – from two men to one and the first introduction of capital equipment – a horse and a sled.

The first recorded use of this device was in 1552 when it was known, in Old English, as a *Drage* from the German word *Trage*, meaning a handbarrow. This word eventually developed to form the word 'Dray' and by 1581 the name was in common use, especially by brewers, to describe a low cart without sides for carrying heavy loads.

This kind of dray was very primitive and it seems strange that, whilst wheels had been around for centuries, they were not – at least to start with – widely used for this type of

short-distance work, as one obvious reason was the poor state of the roads. As late as 1850, many of the roads in what is now suburban Surrey, or even Greater London, were impassable for four months of the year. Contemporary accounts describe coaches and waggons abandoned in about three feet of mud and whole communities which were totally isolated during the winter. In *A Tale of Two Cities*, Charles Dickens describes passengers walking alongside the Dover Mail as the horses struggled through the mud up Shooter's Hill at Blackheath.

There are two views about why the roads were in such a poor state. One is that they were simply not maintained because they carried so little traffic; the other is that they carried so *much* traffic that it was impossible, with existing technology, to maintain them in a satisfactory state of repair. It is quite likely that, up to the time of McAdam, both were true to different degrees in different areas at different times!

By the end of the 16th and into the 17th century, heavy goods tended to be sent by coastal navigation, and lighter goods by packhorse. It was not really until the 17th century that road transport came into being on any scale and, apart from local transport of grain and other agricultural produce,

A single-horse dray, used for delivering bottled beer in cases. This fine example is still in occasional use, drawn by a grey Shire of some 17 hands height. It is only used now for advertising and publicity, since its running cost far exceeds that of a motor vehicle. The lining-in on the chassis longitudinals and cross-bearers draws attention to the cartwright's skills in chamfering, which serves to reduce the unladen weight of the vehicle without materially affecting its strength. Note the drayman's uniform, with the once-familiar 'billycock' hat.

this was predominantly to feed the rapidly growing canal network and the coastal ports. An early entrant to the field was Pickfords, who ran 16 and 18-horse waggons from London to Carlisle, carrying up to 5 tons and taking a week for the journey.

Other reasons for the late introduction of the wheel in some areas may have been that the skills of the wheelwright and the blacksmith, which were required to construct a satisfactory spoked wheel, may not always have been readily to hand. Also, the necessary materials (elm for the nave or hub, oak for the spokes and ash for the felloes or rim-pieces) may only have been available at the right quality at relatively high cost. Given the opportunity, it is worth examining the construction of old iron-tyred wheels: the precision of the offset, tapered mortise and tenon joints, whose measurements were judged by the eye of the wheelwright, are really quite marvellous.

However, to return to the subject of transporting beer: the earliest *wheeled* transport employed was a development of the sled in which the sidemembers were extended to

form shafts. Heavy wheels, 3ft 6in (1,070mm) in diameter and with 6½in (165mm) wide tyres were fitted, and a pair of horses, in tandem, was used to draw loads of around two tons. An oil painting by G Garrard hanging at Southill Park, Bedfordshire, illustrates such a vehicle, which would have been in use up to about 1820. The term 'in tandem' is used to denote the fact that the horses were one behind the other rather than paired side-by-side.

About the same time, to obtain even higher payloads, one or two horses were employed to draw a converted agricultural wain or waggon. Initially, these waggons were hardly adapted at all and were simply used as a flat platform vehicle to which were fitted minor accessories to enable a barrel-skid to be used for loading and unloading across the tailboard. A barrel-skid, incidentally, is a piece of equipment which can still be seen in use today. It consists of two parallel joists of wood joined by curved iron struts. At one end of the joists is a flattened hook which slots in behind a bar on the back, or side, of the vehicle so that casks can be lowered gently to the ground. Barrel-skids

A typical 19th century barrel-dray, sometimes called a brewer's box-van. The braking 'spragg' is just visible tucked up behind the coil of rope which was used for lowering casks into cellars. When climbing steep hills, the spragg was unchained and allowed to drag along the road. If the horses paused for a break, the dray would run back, forcing the spike into the road surface, thus assisting the wooden block-brake to hold the dray stationary. As they moved off, the spike would simply dislodge itself and continue dragging along the road. This was simple, but effective, as was the additional downhill brake known as the 'drugg' or drag-shoe, depending upon which part of the country you are in. In its simplest form this was a block of wood attached to the dray by a chain which, on steep descents, was placed in front of one of the back wheels, preventing it from turning and acting as a very efficient brake. Later forms used a cast-iron channel which performed the same task.

Note also the exposed hinge to the tailboard which allows the hooks on the end of the barrel-skid to be latched on even when the tailboard is lowered.

were – and are – stowed underneath the bed of the vehicle. Other minor fitments might have included a decent-sized hook on which to hang the cellar ropes. Heavy casks are lowered into cellars by looping a rope round them and lowering them down a permanently fixed barrel-skid into the pub's cellar. This is hard, heavy work, even when done slowly; performed quickly, modern draymen can wear out a pair of industrial working gloves in one day! It is small wonder that short cuts are taken – in spite of the potential danger with such heavy items – and casks are slid into cellars with their progress being arrested by a bump-bag at the bottom.

Later waggons were further adapted to improve payload even more by removing the floorboards, except between the centre two longitudinals, with the result that not only was tare weight reduced, thus allowing extra payload, but the barrels could lie comfortably on their sides, or 'on the bouge'.

Although probably not seen simply as productivity improvements at the time – the word 'productivity' had not

Another barrel-dray, of the type known as a 'Mary-Ann' in the workshops. Whitbread in the early Eighties maintained a valuable collection of historic drays and employed a skilled wheelwright and a cartwright to carry out all the necessary maintenance and repair tasks on them. As a pastime these two men built, 'from the wheels up', a replica Mary Ann using no drawings and only measurements made from an existing dray. The replica contained one original component – the metalwork for the drayman's seat, which had been found at the back of a shed. The name Mary-Ann was coined because the original of this type operated out of the Mary-Ann brewery in the Channel Islands.

been invented – many other refinements were gradually embodied. Chassis longitudinals and axle-trees were chamfered to improve their appearance as well as to reduce weight – and increase payload for a given total weight – without materially affecting strength.

Brakes were improved to a degree of sophistication which, for their time, was comparable with today's three-line braking systems. For normal braking on the flat, a shaped, wooden brake-shoe operated on the iron tyre of the vehicle. For downhill braking a drag-shoe, or 'drugg', usually wedge-shaped but occasionally channel-shaped and made of cast iron, was thrown under the wheel causing it to slide and hence slow progress. For uphill braking – to prevent the waggon running backwards when the horses paused for breath – there was a 'spragg'. This was an iron-tipped ash stick attached to a short chain, which trailed behind the waggon and dug into the road as soon as the vehicle started to roll backwards. It was not unknown for waggons to somersault over the spragg if the driver had left things rather late to throw it down. If this happened, all was lost!

These fixtures replaced the earlier methods which relied on the horses to slow down, supplemented by a hook on the end of a chain which was thrown into the wheel to catch a spoke, thus causing the wheel to slide.

These simple two and four-wheeled drays remained in use for many years for short-haul and lighter work but, in the 18th century, the barrel-dray, sometimes called the brewer's box-van, of which the 19th century 'Mary-Ann' is a variant, was introduced. This was a purpose-built dray with iron tyres on which the driver, resplendent in his billycock hat, sat well clear of the payload of some 1½ to 2 tons. Some years ago a replica of one of these fine machines was built in London by an old craftsman who had found the metal parts which surround the drayman's seat. When asked

to show the drawings from which he was working, he disclosed that he had none and was 'copying by eye' from an old, rather dilapidated, original! Some of these beautiful drays – and the replica – are maintained as publicity vehicles by some of the major brewers and can be seen at county fairs and at the Horse of the Year Show.

The subject of horse-drawn transport cannot be left without a word about the motive power itself. Draught horses must be amongst the loveliest of animals; they are huge – weighing about a ton – powerful, and as gentle as it is possible to imagine. Brewers used several different breeds, apart from Shires, whose name seems to have been adopted almost as the generic term for heavy horses. In Britain, the main alternative breeds were Clydesdales – also widely used in farming – Percherons – descendants of the armoured knight's steed – and Suffolk Punches. Each breed has its own characteristics and its own perceived advantages and disadvantages for different types of work.

Early in the morning these beautiful animals would be backed between the shafts and would stand, gently pawing the ground and occasionally striking sparks from their great iron shoes, their warm breath sending clouds of steam into the air. It seems that many horses, but especially those known to the writer, have a particular liking for mints with holes in them and it was a constant pleasure to yield up some mints in return for an affectionate nuzzling. On view amongst many interesting exhibits at the Shire Horse Centre, near Reading, is evidence of the farrier's work, with examples of special horseshoes for those which had special requirements – much like built-up boots. Many breweries employed a full time farrier or blacksmith and until quite recently, one London brewer still shod the Metropolitan Police's horses as a gesture of goodwill.

Drays, as the horses themselves were sometimes called, usually worked in pairs which were matched for appearance,

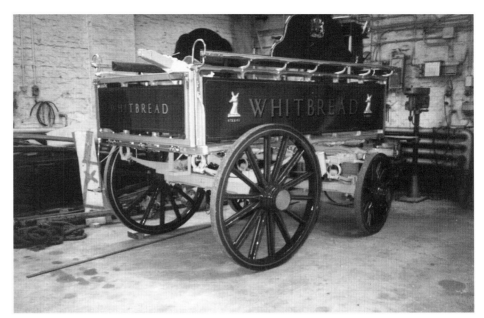

The typical 19th century British brewer's dray was built so robustly that some are still in use today, and the Mary-Ann illustrated is now so valuable that it is confined to show-work. Construction is of oak and ash, and of particular interest are the wheels, which are works of art. Starting with the 'nave' or hub, which is turned from elm, the spokes – made of oak – are mortised into offset, tapered tenons, each being a perfect drive fit. The rim, made of ash felloes or sections, is then fitted carefully to the spokes to give a perfect circle. The iron tyre is shrink-fitted, by first heating it, then placing it over the wheel and allowing it to contract as it cools. The jobs of the cartwright and wheelwright are very highly skilled and there are now few men left who could build a dray 'from the wheels up'.

Another interesting detail on these drays are the springs, which hardly differ in appearance from those on more modern vehicles. Also note the spike-brake or 'spragg'.

Right: A sadly damaged rough proof of a handsome barrel-dray operated by Young's brewery, Wandsworth, in the mid-Thirties. The barrels are stacked 'on the bouge' – sometimes also called stacking 'on the roll'. The load is heavy, hence the need for three horses – the so-called 'Unicorn' configuration – compared with the usual two. The leading horse, often called the cock-horse or steamer, is attached to the dray by a 'single whippletree' connected to the front of the harness pole. As with everything connected with horse-drawn transport, regional names abound for all the various parts and whippletrees were also known as 'whiffletrees', 'swing bars', 'eveners' and as single, double and triple 'trees'. They consisted of a horizontal bar made either of wood or metal which was attached to the trace chains to even out the load for horses working in teams.

Below: A number of covered drays shown in use in the Thirties. Drays of this type are still in use around London, but as much for reasons of publicity than economy as horse drays are nowadays much more expensive to run than motor drays. This is because horses require the attention of groomsmen and stable lads on seven days per week; they require feeding, watering, cleaning and exercising, and the skills required for managing them are increasingly scarce. There can be no doubt, though, that they are attractive and, presumably, must be worthwhile from an advertising viewpoint, although it is likely that sentiment also plays a part.

An excessively decorated dray of the continental pattern, having all wheels the same, or nearly the same size. A feature of equi-rotal waggons, carts and drays was their high deck-height, necessary to allow the front axle's wheels to pass under the body. This rendered them unsuitable for most types of brewery work where heavy weights have to be manhandled, and it has been a feature of brewery vehicle design to the present day that efforts have been made to keep deck or bed-heights as low as possible. Photographed outside Tuborg's offices in Denmark, the umbrella and fancy livery are decidedly 'not as original'.

power and temperament, but not necessarily age. Matching is a skilled business as the coat of a foal will more than likely be different from its adult coat, so buying and breeding called for almost as much skill and experience as building the waggon itself.

By the end of the horse-drawn era, productivity, measured in terms of payload, had increased from under 4cwt to over 1½ tons.

Young & Co's head horse-keeper, Peter Tribe, with two of the famous Young's Brewery Shires pulling the 'Chrome van', photographed outside The Guinea public house in Berkeley Square, London. The dray itself, which was built by Blanche's of Chelsea and is now used mostly for show-work, derives its name from the fact that it is very heavily dressed with chromium-plated fittings. It was obtained, second-hand, from Flowers Brewery when they ceased making horse-drawn deliveries and is almost identical to the Mary-Ann. The horses' working day starts at 5am, when they are given their first feed and grooming begins. Around 6am another bucket of feed is given, grooming is finished, and harnessing begins. Each dray is drawn, or pulled, by a pair of horses and four pairs are sent out each day, so there are eight horses to be prepared. At 7am the draymen arrive to take their horses out; hooves are oiled and the drays attached. Usually, two of the drays will have been loaded with bottles and the other two with casks, which will be delivered within a three-mile radius of the brewery, returning up to three times during the day to reload! The horses are usually given nose-bags, which encourage them to stand patiently whilst a delivery is in progress.

A fine pair of grey Shires at the Whitbread brewery in Faversham, Kent. These gentle creatures weigh over a ton apiece and stand 17 to 18 hands high. A hand is equal to four inches – approximately the width of a man's hand across the knuckles – so they stand about 6ft high at the shoulder. Other heavy horse breeds, apart from Shires, are also used for draught work, amongst which, in Britain, are Clydesdales, Percherons and Suffolk Punches.

Tail-docking used to be quite common until, in the Fifties, it became illegal. Today there is some difference of opinion about whether the tail should be trimmed or left long: whilst tails look better when they are long there is the risk that they may catch in the forecarriage, or that a swishing tail will sweep the reins from the driver's hands; short tails are also claimed by their proponents to be more hygienic.

Each pair of horses must be carefully matched for size, appearance, power and temperament. They are often named in pairs, such as Time and Tide, Gog and Magog, Hercules and Horsa, but these 'official' names, inscribed on their harness, are quite different from their stable, or pet, names. This is so that they are not distracted by passers-by calling them, this being particularly important in modern day processional work such as the Lord Mayor's Show, in which brewery horses play a large part.

An interesting working shot of a drayman – Joe House, of Young's Brewery – unloading a wooden cask from the 'Belgian dray' outside the Green Man public house at Putney, South London. He is using a barrel-skid, which is usually stowed under the bed of the vehicle between deliveries to lower the cask to the ground; a similar skid is often permanently fixed under the cellar-flap outside the pub to enable the casks to be lowered to the cellar. This Bonallack-built dray was obtained for the princely sum of £30 from Mann & Crossman, the London brewers situated in the East End, when they ceased horse-drawn deliveries. Its estimated value is in excess of £20,000 and expert opinion believes that a dray of this quality could not, today, be built for this sum! It is known as the Belgian dray because it is of continental appearance – having equi-rotal wheels – and did, in fact, visit Belgium on a publicity outing in the Seventies. On the dray can be seen the cellar-rope, the nose-bags and the chrome-plated 'pins' which prevent the barrels rolling off the back of the waggon whilst in motion. The chock-brake serves as confirmation that the wheel is steel-tyred as it is not feasible to use this type of brake on rubber tyres – even solid ones.

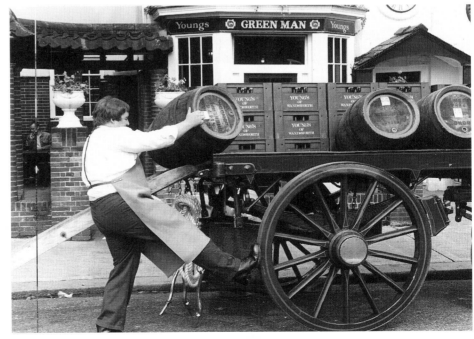

19

A modern day photograph showing six of Young's drays engaged in the winning of a bet. The bet was that horse-drawn drays could not cope with present day large deliveries as far afield as Wimbledon (from Wandsworth, in South London). Three standard flats and three of Young's own design – and quite recent – covered-cab drays are seen here delivering the goods – and collecting the bet. Young's of Wandsworth are now the only brewers in London still using dray horses for daily deliveries. The horses are on the road five days a week, delivering real ales to pubs in the Wandsworth, Putney and Battersea areas as they have done for almost 300 years – a tradition which only a handful of breweries in the whole country can still boast. Standing on the nearside of the leading dray is David Dunn, who is responsible for painting the Young's and many of the Whitbread show drays.

Unladen weight of this vehicle is about 25cwt (1,275kg) and payload is up to about 3 tons although, at least until Whitbread stopped using horses for London deliveries in 1990, the horses were not overworked, being given just about enough work to keep them fit. Note that the wheels are 'equi-rotal' or of equal size, which was at one time an almost universal feature. Wheels of different size – with the front ones being smaller – were introduced to improve the 'lock' as the smaller wheels could pass under the load platform. The modern horse-drawn dray is 'equi-rotal' partly because of the convenience of having a single tyre size and partly because the suspension is sufficiently sophisticated to raise the platform to the desired working height. The size of the wheel is dictated by the size of the drum or disc brake required to meet the present day Construction and Use Regulations which allow for air-suspension to lower the deck for unloading.

This single-horse dray, photographed in the London workshops in 1981, is a fine example of its type but, in many respects, betrays its early origins as a farm-waggon derivative. The excessively decorative seat would, though, have been very out of place in an agricultural environment and the width of the iron tyres suggests road, rather than field, operation. London once boasted several waggon and cart builders and repairers, and examples of Bonallack's and Blanche's work are illustrated in this book. Another major builder was Whitmee, who had premises at what was Brewers Lane at Putney Bridge and at York Road, Wandsworth, where they produced a special purpose 'knacker's cart' with high sides and a small winch operating through a trapdoor at the front. The back of the cart formed a long ramp for loading.

20

Photographed about 1970, one team stands harnessed and ready for their day's work while others stand by awaiting loading and hitch-up. Once the drays have left the brewery to make their deliveries, an enormous amount of work still remains to be done. Loose boxes and stalls must be mucked out and spare horses must be watered and fed. Show horses need exercising during the day in the schooling ring and, at this brewery, there is also a Dorset Horn ram, the brewery mascot, to be cared for. It is not difficult to see why mechanical transport, which did not need 24 hours a day attention, was so attractive to so many operators in the early part of the century. On grounds of purely transport economics it seems unlikely that horse-drawn drays are a paying proposition in the Nineties, but from the marketing and publicity point of view they certainly seem popular.

Amongst other brewers still using horses for transport are Adnams in the South Wold, who have two pairs of Percherons, Tetley's of Leeds, with several pairs of grey Shires, Vaux Brewery, Sunderland and Wadsworth's of Devizes in Wiltshire. Courage formerly used horses in Bristol, Reading and London, where two breweries were situated, one at Anchor Terrace, near Southwark Bridge, and one at Butler's Wharf, near Tower Bridge, where in the mid-Eighties the rings were still in the wall where the horses were once tethered. Whitbread retained horse-drawn deliveries in London for many years after the brewery had moved away but, eventually, bringing beer into London to be transshipped onto horse-drawn drays for delivery proved totally uneconomic.

Below: The George Inn must have had more to commend it than its rather dreary appearance would suggest. This enormous delivery, which appears to be of five butts and five hogsheads, amounting to over 800 gallons of 'Fine Rigden's Ales' plus whatever is in the carboys and demijohns, would need to be consumed fairly quickly for the beer to remain in peak condition. The draymen and the publican look pleased with themselves, but there are some wistful expressions on some of the other faces.

The dray is, again, not especially typical of the period, having more the appearance of a coal 'lurry' – the old word for lorry. It is quite likely that the different trades interchanged their transport to meet seasonal trading peaks then, as they do now. Beer and coal, having roughly opposite peak delivery seasons, made ideal transport companions. The summer shadows in the photograph add weight to this hypothesis, as does the fact that Rigdens was a Kentish brewery supplying, no doubt, the needs of the Kent coalfield miners.

Note the skid-hooks over the wheels; most unloading was over the tail of the vehicle, using a barrel-skid, but on long-bed drays a facility was required for side unloading. Also note the downhill skid-buffer, or drag-shoe.

Charlie Butler and Steve. This is the original photograph from which the inn sign for The Charlie Butler was taken. Charlie was the head horsekeeper at Young's Brewery, Wandsworth for many years and is the only living 'commoner' ie non-royalty, to have given his name to a pub. There have always been horses at the Ram Brewery, which was established in the 17th century and taken over by Young in 1831. Today more than 20 horses are kept there – most of them Shires, the biggest breed of all and of which Steve is an example. There are also two Suffolk Punches – the only ones in the brewing industry – and two Percherons. The prince of the Shires is Goliath, who was born in 1977 and measures 19 hands 1½in (6ft 5½in or 1.97m) from hoof to withers. He is listed in the *Guinness Book of Records* as the tallest horse in Britain.

Photographed at the Shires Spring Show at Peterborough showground in 1991, Young's 'Brass van' is about to enter the arena with the head horsekeeper driving. As with the 'Chrome van', the Brass van was so called because of the amount of decorative brass used in its construction. The use of original brass informs us that the van was always intended for 'best' use, right from the time it was supplied by Blanche's of Chelsea. Heavy horse shows have, in recent years, increased in popularity to the extent that at the 1991 East of England Show there were no less than 32 pairs, combined at various times into 14 four-horse and 14 three-horse teams. This compares with a few years ago when six pairs would have been a good turnout!

Regional brewers occasionally ran brewery outings – usually a trip to the countryside or, where distance permitted, the seaside. This very old and faded photograph, believed to have been taken in Epsom High Street, dates from the early part of this century.

CHAPTER TWO

The Steam Era

During the 19th century, development of horse-drawn drays was slow and even the modern version, which can be seen on the streets of some cities today, differs relatively little from the early waggon types of the 18th century, apart from the addition of pneumatic tyres.

Perhaps there was little incentive to improve; roads, whilst congested in cities, were in ever improving condition and, thanks to the efforts of Macadam and Telford, labour was also plentiful. Productivity was up from two men handling 36 gallons (in the 16th century) to two men (and two horses) handling some 2 tons – approximately 10 barrels or 360 gallons, a tenfold improvement in manpower productivity!

However, with the introduction of self-propelled transport, brewers – possibly together with millers and coal-merchants – came to the forefront of the development of heavy transport. All of these trades were early entrants to the field of steam traction and it is on record that brewers were, in fact, amongst the first to place the load *upon* the vehicle rather than having the vehicle draw a separate, loaded trailer as was the common practice with traction engines.

Whilst in 1828 there is evidence of the Frenchman, Pecqueur, having applied for a patent for a steam-propelled load-carrying vehicle, there is only doubtful evidence that it was ever built. It was much later in the 19th century that steam came to be applied to free-ranging self-propelled traction, although of course it had been in use for many years on the canals where stationary engines hauled waggon-trains and trams up inclined planes as an adjunct to the canal system. Gravity assisted the process by using the weight of the empty waggons on the way down.

Earliest of the road-going steam vehicles in general use were the overtype traction engines, similar in appearance to a railway locomotive and with the engine *over* the boiler, the feature which gave it its name. Overtypes usually hauled a laden trailer with payloads in the 3 to 5-ton bracket.

Two men were required to work these vehicles; one, a skilled man, to drive the vehicle on which steering, braking and driver's visibility left much to be desired, and the other to stoke the boiler, act as mate and assist with the deliveries. This introduced a sort of class system, with the drayman as boss and the trouncer as dogsbody.

Casks were heavy and cumbersome and required two men to handle them at the destination so, at this stage, manpower appears to have reached the bare minimum for brewery delivery work of two men per dray and this was to persist for a very long time.

Popular as steam became in Britain, where abundant and cheap supplies of coal were to be had, it never caught on in the same way – at least, so early – in Europe or the USA. Early interest in steam for transport in Britain was motivated by enormous increases in the cost of fodder for horses at the time of the Napoleonic wars. It remained popular in Britain in the brewing, milling and coal trades which had heavy loads to carry, with loads of over 4 tons being catered for by steam and supplemented by horses, right up to 1918 and beyond. Brewers, of course, had years of experience of steam engineering as steam had played an important role in the production process at the brewery.

For all but the very heaviest of loads, traction engines, which drew a separate trailer, eventually gave way to steam-waggons which had the load placed upon them. About this time the word 'lorry' started to come into more general use, although it had been around since the early 19th century, possibly as a derivation of the name 'Lawrie'. Lawrie was a spare time inventor and was responsible for the design of a particular type of tub-cart, or tram, running initially on plateways and later on railways for carrying coal from the mines. In time the name came to mean any heavy load-carrying vehicle. It is also thought that the name corrupted to 'lurry', but this may be a regional pronunciation of the

This view inside the Thornycroft factory at Basingstoke in 1900 shows what look like 5-ton 'Colonials' under construction. These were popular exports, particularly to the Empire, but also enjoyed quite a strong home demand.

Thornycroft, together with Leyland, were the earliest producers of steam waggons in any recognizable volume and, in 1898, Thornycroft were the first manufacturer ever to produce an 'artic', or articulated vehicle, in which a semi-trailer imposed part of its load on the drawing vehicle. The semi-trailer in this case had two axles, but Thornycroft were well ahead of their time and the idea did not catch on for many years.

In 1902, Thornycroft started producing internal combustion engined vehicles and their success, at least with petrol engines, led to their abandoning steam as a source of power in 1907. Later Thornycroft diesel engines were never rated by operators, only being considered useful for marine applications, where they functioned virtually at constant revs.

Thornycroft were vigorous exporters as this 1900 model, operating in France, shows. Whilst generally similar to the Colonial, the vehicle illustrated appears to have a longer wheelbase which might indicate that it was not originally purchased for brewery work. Long wheelbases allow extra load to be placed on the platform and, with beer being such a heavy product, it seems unlikely that a 'stretched' chassis would have been bought for this work.

There appear to be 12 hogsheads and 18 barrels on this load which, if full, would have weighed around 15 tons! It says much for the driver's skill and confidence – or ignorance – that he would take out a load such as this with only wood-block brakes on the wheels. He would, though, also have had the facility of 'reverse steam' to assist the process!

Note the coiled hose stowed behind the rear wheel; this was for 'watering-up' en route.

This Foden 4-tonner, although operated in Kent, was registered early in 1904 in Cheshire, the home of Foden, whose works were at Sandbach. Its general condition, particularly the tyres, suggest that it is brand new. All brasswork was kept beautifully polished as depot inspectors might descend at any time and, after checking the petty cash, would examine the condition of the vehicles. Anything less than spotless would result in a crew being taken off the road for a few days for a spot of inside work in the warehouse, resulting in a loss of status – and pay.

In 1907, Foden ran an advertisement comparing steam power with horse power. Obviously, since Foden were running the advert, steam came out markedly cheaper, but it is interesting to see by how much. Two 'motors' and four drivers cost £582 per annum compared with £1,014 for the equivalent *load* capacity with horses. The steam waggons, £600 each new, compared with horses, even then, at £70 each. The wages of the 'carmen' (for horse transport) were 28s (£1.40) per week whilst the motor drivers earned 35s (£1.75).

word or even an alternative derivation whose ancestry is unknown.

At the beginning of the 20th century came the undertype waggons in which the cylinders and valve-gear were mounted beneath the boiler, making them look much more like the lorries of today. Many famous names were associated with steam from these early days, some of which survived in a major way and went on to become producers of motor lorries. Amongst these were firms like Foden, Sentinel, Atkinson, Leyland and several others who became absorbed into larger or more successful companies. The rate of fall-out can be judged from the fact that during the 20-year period bridging the turn of the century between 70 and 80 manufacturers were engaged in building steam vehicles.

R W Kinder, in his book *The First Hundred Road Motors*, introduces a very useful classification of steam waggons into eight main types, which are broadly as follows:

Type A. Undertype with the boiler behind the front axle and the driver behind the boiler. This type was produced by such firms as Londonderry, Stewart and Thornycroft, roughly between 1898 and 1905.

Type B. Another undertype with a similar layout to Type A but with the driver in front of the boiler. These were produced by Carters, Coulthard, English, Halley and Hercules around 1900 to 1906.

Type C. Also similar to Type A but with the boiler ahead of the front axle so that the driver's view of the road was again obscured by the boiler! Many firms adopted this layout, mainly between 1900 and 1910, amongst which were Bayley, Garrett, Jesse Ellis, Lifu, Leyland, Robertson, Robey, SM, St Pancras, Sentinel, Straker, Thames and Wantage.

Type D. Undertype but with a *locomotive*-style boiler and the driver standing beside it. Produced around 1899 to 1909 by Bretherton & Bryan and Mann.

Type E. Undertype again, with the driver standing *behind* a short horizontal boiler. Built by Allchin, Beyer Peacock, Foster, Hindley, Mann, Stewart, Straker and Thornycroft from about 1905 to 1909.

Type F. The first of the overtypes, with the driver standing behind a locomotive-style boiler. This type featured from about 1901 to 1927 and was built by such companies as Allchin, Aveling & Porter, Burrell, Clayton, Foden, Foster, Garrett, Mann, Ransomes, Robey, Sentinel, Straker, Tasker and Wallis & Steevens.

Type G. Basically a continuation of and improvement to the Type C undertype, but with an enclosed cab. This style was built by firms such as Atkinson, Clayton, Fowler, Garrett, Leyland, Robey and Sentinel from about 1911 to 1930 and is, by any standards, identifiable with later forward-control motor lorries.

Type H. Probably the ultimate in steam lorry design, the Type H undertype is a revival of the Type B with an enclosed and, occasionally, quite streamlined and modern-looking cab and bodywork. Available from about 1930 to the end of the steam era in 1939, these were built by the only two manufacturers effectively to survive that long – Foden and Sentinel.

Initially, steam lorries and drays were available as four-wheeled vehicles which had a relatively restricted load-space – although, on the undertypes, this was much less so than on the earlier overtype waggons. In an attempt to improve productivity further by placing even greater loads on the vehicle, experiments were carried out around 1927 – notably by Sentinel – in which an extra axle was added under an extended load platform, and so the first *commercial* six-wheeler was born. These were not used on any great scale for deliveries to public houses but brewers did use them for some of the heavier work, including the transport of 'spent' wet barley grains and for transfer or trunking work. Whilst

This beautiful shot shows two styles of Sentinel undertype steam waggon. Registered in Bristol in the early Twenties, HT 9726 is a *Super* Sentinel with the new, stylish cab and improved-design wheels, whilst AW 6176 is a postwar *Standard* Sentinel. Much was learned about wheel design for road vehicles during the First World War and this is an interesting comparison between the old and the new. The photo was taken in the early morning whilst raising steam, and the crews can be seen cleaning and polishing their vehicles before setting out for the day's work. The fact that the loads are covered with a canvas tilt suggests that this might be wintertime so, whilst waiting the 50 minutes or so required to raise steam, some fairly vigorous sort of work could be done to keep warm. The older vehicle was registered in Shropshire, Sentinel's home county with their works at Shrewsbury. In the days before vehicle transporters it was fairly common practice for manufacturers to register vehicles before delivery so that they could be driven to their eventual place of work. Note the AA badges, themselves a collector's piece today!

Sentinel were major British manufacturers of steam lorries and were in business from 1906 until 1956, by which time they were producing 'oil-engined' (diesel) vehicles, but not very successfully. The company started as Alley & McLellan in Polmadie, Glasgow but moved to Shrewsbury in 1917. After several changes of name over the years, most of them fairly subtle, they ceased trading in 1956 as Sentinel (Shrewsbury) Ltd.

The model illustrated, the 1906 Standard Sentinel, is thus one of their earliest models, having iron-tyred wheels. However, slightly unusual for the time was the employment of Ackerman steering – the type found on modern vehicles – in which the wheels steer at the end of the axle without the axle moving from its normal, transverse position. The Standard Sentinel had a vertical boiler with cross-water tubes and was capable of producing 150deg Fahrenheit of 'superheat'. Superheating is a process in steam engineering in which the steam is reheated, usually by passing additional heating tubes through the boiler's exhaust gases. This results in any remaining water vapour being converted to steam, thus raising its pressure as well as ensuring that the steam is 'dry'.

The Standard Sentinel continued in production, with various improvements – including the addition of solid rubber tyres – until the introduction of the Super Sentinel in 1923.

This preserved Foden overtype was photographed at the Minehead Steam Fair in the west of England in 1982. Starkey, Knight and Ford were West Country brewers so it seems likely that this did not have to go far to find a restorer, who has done an excellent job on it. Claimed to be of about 1904 vintage, it is impossible to confirm this from its number-plate since Cheshire – where the Foden was both made and registered – lost all their registration records for the period from December 1903 to August 1917! The body is slightly unusual in that only the centre section of the strake-sided body is hinged, the remainder being fixed. The topboard, though, extends the length of the body so that when it is lowered it protects the vehicle as well as providing a step-up on to the vehicle. The offside mirror does not look original and probably has more to do with present-day Construction and Use Regulations than it does with historic accuracy.

Left: This 1911 steamer of Rigden's, Faversham, is typical of Foden's principal product of the period, the 4-ton overtype steam lorry. Following early efforts with undertype (engine under boiler) vehicles, Foden built their first overtype in 1900. In this, they used a launch-type boiler, but this was soon discarded in favour of the much more conventional locomotive-style boiler with which Foden had great success in the 1901 War Office trials.

Final drive on early versions was taken from the gear-shaft to the back axle differential by two roller chains in tandem, since no single roller chain could be found which was strong enough to transmit the power. This resulted in frequent breakages because, in practice, it proved impossible to maintain equal tension on both chains, so that one or the other would take the whole load and snap. Around 1909 suitably strong single chain was developed and later models were fitted thus, as shown in the photograph. The design then remained basically unchanged until 1925, by which time undertypes were being successfully used. By the end of the First World War, some 800 Foden overtypes were in military service and a number survive today.

This photograph shows quite clearly the compound cylinders mounted on top of the boiler, ahead of the flywheel, with the twin safety valves and steam whistle between them.

these were the first commercial six-wheelers, they were not the first vehicles to employ three axles on a rigid chassis. In 1923, experiments had been carried out in conjunction with the War Office to develop a vehicle with good cross-country ability. The trials were carried out on a four-wheel-drive motor lorry and were the subject of a lecture to the Institute of Automobile Engineers by Captain R K Hubbard, OBE, RASC, in 1925.

Foden introduced the overtype steam waggon as early as 1900 or 1901 to overcome problems of access with the earlier undertypes. Undertypes also suffered, in the early days, with problems of boiler reliability and the more conventional locomotive-type boiler was used to take advantage of tried and proven technology. The designations 'overtype' and 'undertype' refer to the position of the 'engine' – the cylinders and valve-gear – in relation to the boiler. Thus, an overtype had the cylinders over the boiler and the undertype had all 'the works' beneath the boiler.

By 1912, Foden had established a first-class reputation and some operators owned large fleets as this scene, showing 4-tonners at Isleworth brewery, demonstrates.

This slightly unusual vehicle is fitted with a crossflow boiler which very few manufacturers tried – and hardly any with any degree of success. The advantage of a crossflow boiler was that in hilly areas, all the water-tubes remained submerged so there was a much reduced risk of boiling dry, or of 'dumping' the boiler's contents into the fire – a safety device which was used to prevent boiler explosions.

The idea of a crossflow boiler was patented jointly by G W Mann of Leeds, and J Clayton, the steam waggon builder. The Yorkshire Patent Steam Wagon Company produced vehicles like this at Hunslet, Leeds, between 1903 and 1928 and the photograph may have been taken to demonstrate the enormous load potential being offered. Counting up the load and assuming all the casks are full indicates a load of around 18 tons on the combined 'waggon and drag', the brewery slang for a drawbar-trailer combination.

The model shown, which is almost certainly a Yorkshire, appears to be from about 1913, the dating being by reference to the type of wheels fitted. Only about four brewers ever used Yorkshires and all of these were in the north of England.

One of the reasons six-wheelers were not used for delivery work was the difficulty in keeping axle loadings legal once load had been removed from the back of the platform. When fully laden the load carried behind the back axle had a counterbalancing, see-saw effect so that the front axle load was within legal tolerances. As soon as the counterbalance was removed by taking load off the back of

Left: The very earliest steam waggons were undertypes but, around the turn of the century, overtypes started to gain in popularity since they avoided problems of access and boiler unreliability. Like so many technological innovations, some manufacturers continued with the old ways – and often improved upon them – while others took up the new ideas and introduced their own. Garrett was a very innovative firm in so far as engineering was concerned, even though, for 1916, there is nothing very special about this 5-ton overtype, operated by the Sheffield brewers, Tennant Brothers. It is equipped with chain steering and cast wheels, which are, at least, fitted with rubber tyres. Barely discernible on the side of the cab is the information that the unladen weight is just over 4 tons, whilst the laden weight is distributed approximately 6 tons on the rear axle and 3 tons on the front.

Garrett experimented with many different types, but returned to the undertype in 1922. This was a very advanced model incorporating a new boiler which bore so many resemblances to the one used by Sentinel at the time that the matter came close to litigation for infringement of patent.

Whilst not used by brewers to any great extent for delivery work, traction engines would have been used for the movement of 'spent grains' – what is left of the barley after the fermentation process – as an important ingredient of animal feeds.

This photograph of a Garrett traction engine of about 1917 vintage clearly illustrates one of the difficulties with the control of early, pre-Ackerman steered, vehicles. Steering was effected by rapidly turning a steering wheel which wound a chain onto a drum, thus pulling one side or the other of the front axle. Thus, the whole axle-beam moved whilst the wheels themselves simply rotated at their ends.

However, once a turn had been made, rapid winding of the steering wheel in the opposite direction was necessary to take off the lock and, once off, the next turn had to be prepared for by taking up the slack in the chain in readiness for winding on lock again. Braking, in the main, was carried out by using a little reverse steam so a driver would be kept very busy – occasionally with unhappy results as the picture shows!

the vehicle, the front axle 'went illegal'. This problem puzzled engineers and operators alike for many years and, eventually, two different but related solutions were found.

One of the solutions adopted was to place a fourth axle at the front of the load platform, close to the front axle, which clearly required that it, too, must be steered. This enabled relatively huge loads to be carried, and eight-wheelers were widely used for long-distance work. Whilst

Another example of the Garrett overtype, BJ 5147 was registered in East Suffolk in 1920 and was operated by the Wolverhampton and Dudley Brewery as Fleet No 15. This model is the 8-tonner and exhibits few external differences in appearance from the 5-tonner. One small improvement, as far as productivity is concerned, is the replacement of the heavier stake-sided body seen on the earlier 3-tonner with the 'boxing-ring' type of body. This body-type was less suitable for the carriage of crates than the stake-sided body and further evidence that this vehicle was, in fact, used for delivering casks is provided by the barrel-skid rail on the mini tailboard.

Weight details, required by contemporary legislation to be painted on the side of the cab, inform us that unladen weight was around 4 tons, with laden weight distributed 4 tons on the front and 8 tons on the back axle.

Similar in appearance to the contemporary steam waggons and lorries is this 5-ton Orwell electric. This is quite an unusual vehicle for brewery work, but provides further evidence that the brewers were always on the look-out for anything which might have some advantage to offer. One of the perceived virtues of the electric vehicle was the fact that it had few, quite simple controls, especially when compared with the steam waggon on which the controls, simple enough in themselves, had to be used with care and skill as mistakes could have dangerous consequences.

Electric vehicles bearing the name Orwell were built by Ransomes, Sims and Jefferies at the Orwell Works at Ipswich, Suffolk between 1915 and 1928. Ransomes were, predominantly, manufacturers of agricultural equipment, their plough manufacturing business dating back as far as 1789 and, as early as 1842, they exhibited a self-propelling engine which could travel at about 4 to 5mph, this possibly being the world's first traction engine. Early Orwells were powered by electric motors on the front hubs but on this model can clearly be seen the drive chain from a centrally mounted motor. Note the large – and heavy – Exide battery pack and the perforated disc wheels which are of comparatively light weight to compensate for the weight of the traction batteries.

The vehicle illustrated, a 20-barrel electric tank lorry dating from September 1929, tipped the scales at 4 ton 5 cwt, unladen and the weight was distributed with 3 tons on the front axle and 6 tons on the rear when fully loaded. The tank casing was supplied by Mortlake.

this development actually took place during the steam era, only nine eight-wheeled steam lorries were ever built. They were designated SDDG8 and were built by Sentinel of Shrewsbury from 1929. For some reason, the eight-wheeler became affectionately known as an 'eight-legger' and it is interesting to conjecture whether Leyland adopted the nickname to launch their Octopus or vice versa.

The alternative method also involved fitting an extra steered axle at the front of the load platform but, in this case, the second axle at the rear of the platform was dispensed with. This configuration, officially called twin-steer but colloquially known as the 'Chinese-six', did not occur until much later, in 1938, with the ERF C15 possibly being the first, some years after steam vehicles had ceased production in any quantity.

By the Thirties the battle for efficiency and productivity was gaining momentum. The opportunity for making major improvements, however, was impaired by the negative attitudes of Parliament and, even in those days, the hostility of the general public towards heavy road transport. It is interesting to observe that the nearest that Parliament has

ever come to a unanimous vote in the House of Commons was when increases in gross vehicle weight were debated. Needless to say, the weights did not get through!

There are many attractive tales from the steam era. Breweries appointed inspectors who would descend unexpectedly upon a depot and, after counting the petty cash, would carry out a vehicle inspection. If vehicles were not spotless, with all the brass brightly polished, drivers went in fear of relegation to trouncer's work for a few weeks.

Their jobs were also at risk for another disciplinary offence. Unlike railway locomotives which run more-or-less on the flat, steam lorries had to contend with hills and one of the features which added a little excitement to the job was fear of 'dumping' a boiler. Inside the boiler, and normally submerged by water when on level ground, was a white-metal plug. If this was exposed, as on a hill, and therefore not cooled by the water, the metal would melt and dump the contents of the boiler on the fire. This, in fact, was a safety device to avoid boiler explosions, but only one chance was allowed! The development of a crossflow boiler

Garrett produced vehicles at Leiston, in Suffolk, between 1856 and 1960, producing in all about 950 steam waggons before going on to manufacture mainly electric vehicles, including trolleybuses.

The Garrett 4-tonner model shown has a number of interesting features: the cab is totally enclosed with a glazed windscreen; rubber tyres are fitted – albeit solid, yet it is fitted with acetylene lighting, which was slightly old-fashioned even in 1923. This is probably a manufacturer's photograph, taken before the vehicle entered service since there is no number-plate. Just behind the door can be seen painted the speed limits applicable to this type of vehicle: 12mph or, with a trailer, 5mph!

Sentinels were always popular with brewers, not only for their power and speed but also for their reliability. This Super Sentinel DDG4 was operated in the north west of England from about 1924. It had two speeds and operated with a boiler pressure of 275psi, compared with the previous model, the Standard Sentinel, which operated at 230psi. This simple statement conceals the fact that some clever engineering had gone into improving the power output whilst reducing the weight. Also on this model, a two-speed 'gearbox', incorporating a differential, was introduced between the crankshaft and a countershaft, with chains at each side driving the rear wheels. This enabled the engine to be run whilst the vehicle was stationary, without disengaging the chains.

Alley & McLellan, the makers of Sentinels, were great innovators with many patents to their name. They were amongst the first to try three axles, and were *the* first to produce an eight-wheeler. They certainly sold more steamers and over a longer period than any other manufacturer and also had the advantage of a first-class service network in Britain. Apart from this their highly efficient steam superheaters enabled them to maintain a good head of steam and they still came out cheaper than most of the competition. The very last steam waggon to be built for the British market was a Sentinel, in 1939, but an export order for Argentina was fulfilled as late as 1950.

by the Yorkshire Steam Wagon Co was a bold and largely successful attempt to overcome this.

Steam engineering makes a fascinating study in its own right, with the small road-going engines having much in common with the huge ocean-going steam engines found in ships. Early road engines were of the simple type, meaning that steam was expanded only once in a single cylinder or, at best, simultaneously in two identical cylinders. Later, compound engines appeared in which the exhaust steam from a high-pressure cylinder was re-used in a lower-pressure cylinder. Unlike marine engines, road engines exhausted their steam to the atmosphere so that large

Only nine of these Sentinel SDDG8s were ever built and this No 9105, built in 1934, is the sole survivor. Seen here at the Historic Commercial Vehicle Society's annual London to Brighton run in May 1986, this vehicle was originally the maker's demonstrator and was later sold to a heavy haulier in South Wales. Whilst few were made, and there are no records of any having been used by brewers, they were the forerunners of a type which became immensely popular in the brewing trade, for long-distance work, where their high payload capacity gained extra productivity by minimizing the number of trips required to transport a given quantity of product. Sentinel were the first manufacturer ever to try an eight-wheeled configuration and their first attempt was the DG8 15-tonner introduced in 1929 following experiments in 1927 with conversions of four-wheelers to six-wheelers. These newer models reverted to the older cross-tube boilers, but at an increased pressure of 275psi, thus allowing cylinder dimensions to be reduced to 6in bore and 8in stroke. Sentinel introduced shaft drive to replace their chain drive in about 1935–6.

quantities of water had to be carried and topping up was not infrequent. In marine engines the steam is condensed back into water for reheating back to steam, but this is not possible for small engines as they cannot economically carry large enough quantities of cooling water; at sea there is plenty of cool water about to do the job!

A contemporary textbook sums up the merits and demerits of steam for road transport as:

Disadvantages:
1 Time and labour of raising steam every day.
2 Need for firing and feed water control on the road.
3 Need for washing out the boiler weekly.
4 Greater tare weight, or non-paying load.
5 Risk of fire from sparks or ashes.
6 Difficulty of men in keeping clean while working.

Advantages:
1 Smooth and quiet working.
2 Flexibility of power and ease of exact control.
3 Large reserve of power, and so fewer gearchanges.
4 Good acceleration.
5 Use of cheap, home-produced fuel.

Given these perceived advantages and disadvantages it is not difficult to see why operators began to prefer other modes but, in fact, a number of other factors also contributed to the decline of the steam lorry. Very few steamers ran on pneumatic tyres and the 1932 Salter Report, together with the prohibitive legislation which was introduced for vehicles with solid tyres, was a definite 'nail in their coffin'. Even those steam vehicles which did run on pneumatics were still much heavier than the motor drays and lorries which by then had become fairly commonplace so, essentially because of their lower productivity, they were phased out.

The final straw was the introduction to Britain, from Germany, of the compression-ignition engine, or 'oiler' attributed to Dr Rudolph Diesel, who was a development engineer with the firm of MAN in Nuremburg. But first the story of the petrol engine must be told.

CHAPTER THREE

Motor Drays

So far horse power and steam power have been discussed almost as if there were no alternatives to them. There has, though, been more than enough choice available for the last 100 years even if in the last quarter of this century we appear to have turned full-circle to the point where choice, at least in terms of motive power, is restricted to diesel engines.

The earliest successful attempts to move away from external combustion, ie using boilers, to internal combustion, involved not diesel, which was not widely used for road transport in Britain – or anywhere else for that matter – until the Thirties, but petrol engines.

Around the turn of the 20th century, this development brought about a decrease in average payload which, on the face of it, seems an unusual development in the search for productivity. Productivity, though, has different meanings for different people, and even *The Concise Oxford Dictionary* has four definitions:

1 the capacity to produce;

2 the quality or state of being productive;

3 the effectiveness of productive effort; and

4 production per unit of effort.

The productivity which the brewers were chasing by improving vehicle designs was the ability to deliver as much beer as possible at the lowest cost consistent with protecting the quality of the product. With this in mind, some of the stranger ideas come into focus and what may appear to be retrograde steps are, in fact, steps along the path toward improvement.

Even so, it seems odd to opt for petrol-powered vehicles when they had a smaller payload than steamers. However, to understand the thinking behind this we need to look at what was happening with beer at the time. Bottled beer, as distinct from cask beer, was becoming more widely accepted and was being sold into outlets other than just public houses, so there was a need to deliver these less heavy loads to what were, quite often, less accessible destinations with something slightly faster and more manoeuvrable. Further, up to the beginning of the First World War there had been a fairly healthy country house trade, supplying beer to the servants' halls, and for shoots at the big country houses. Whilst this diminished markedly during the war, with many of the servants in the services and fewer opportunities for game shooting, such deliveries as were made were ideal for the new motors.

Additionally, brewers were always keen to be seen as progressive, so adoption of emerging technologies was quite desirable for them as evidenced by the fact that, at one time or another, famous engineers like Smeaton, Watt and others as well as chemists – notably Pasteur – were employed by brewers to keep them at the forefront of development.

The early load-carrying petrol-engined vehicles, though, were little more than large passenger cars with a platform placed where the seats would have been. They were neither powerful enough nor sufficiently robust in their construction for the large, heavy loads associated with brewers and, if they were to be adopted by brewery transport chiefs, a different role had to be found for them. So, until they could be developed sufficiently to cater for heavy work they were confined to the light tasks with cask delivery remaining the province of the horse and the steamer. Overloading, however, was commonplace with all types.

An additional productivity advantage was that only one motorman was required to drive the vehicle and he was quite capable of delivering crates single-handed. Not only that, but motormen required far less training than steam waggon drivers so were more readily available in the labour market.

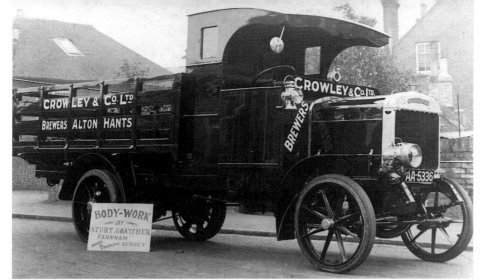

Registered about 1910, this Thornycroft J-type illustrates the earlier use of wheels with cast spokes, this feature being replaced around 1912. This was probably done for the War Department trials as the later dished wheel proved very popular in that quarter. It is interesting to compare this vehicle with the photograph of Perseverance on page 40. The cab is generally much less sophisticated and acetylene lamps have not yet given way to electrics. What might appear to be a very light chain-drive to the rear axle is in fact a brake rod, since Thornycroft were major protagonists of all-gear transmissions.

Starkey, Knight and Ford, the West Country brewers and wine merchants, were clearly very proud of their two new Napier 3-tonners, turning out what looks like most of their office staff as well as drivers and mechanics to be photographed with them. Try allocating jobs to people in the photo – which one was the accountant, for example, and which was the head brewer?

It is not easy to identify the date for these two photos although acetylene lamps suggest prewar rather than postwar. Perhaps the flags and bunting signify something – or perhaps they are just celebrating the arrival of the two new additions to their fleet.

Napiers were not widely used for brewery work even though by 1913 they offered models in the 30cwt, 2-ton and 3-ton categories. They ceased truck production in 1920, except for a brief interlude in 1931 with a design for a mechanical horse, the rights on which were eventually sold to Scammell. After 1913, all their vehicles were offered with four-cylinder engines, magneto ignition, 'unit' transmission and a final worm-drive.

Dennis Brothers Ltd were major suppliers of vehicles to the brewery business well into the Sixties, having set up their vehicle building business in Guildford, Surrey, in 1904. Even before that they had experimented with motorized tricycles, priced at 82 guineas (£86.10) which were, no doubt, a development from their original business – cycle-making. In 1907 they turned to commercial vehicle production, becoming most famous for their fire engines and pumps, although buses – and even lawnmowers – formed a large part of their production. By 1909 Dennis employed around 400 men and were a major local employer and by 1912, the year of the vehicle in the photograph, they had produced over 2,000 commercial chassis.

The model shown is almost certainly the 3-tonner although the 2-tonner, 3-tonner and 4-tonner had many identical features – including wooden wheels. The brass radiator, whose distinctive 'threepenny-bit' shape was retained for many years, was characteristic of Dennis models.

In 1912, with a European war on the horizon, the War Department decided to introduce a subsidy scheme in which civilian vehicle operators were paid sums of money – up to £180 per year – to keep suitable vehicles in a fit state to be commandeered should war break out. There followed a spate of activity by the various vehicle manufacturers to prepare their offerings for the War Office trials which would result in specific makes and models qualifying for the higher levels of subsidy. Particularly successful in these trials were famous names like Leyland and Thornycroft with internal combustion-engined vehicles and Foden with steam waggons. Thornycroft, at one time famous for their high-quality steam waggons, had no entry in the steam trials having sold that side of their business to a Glasgow firm in 1907.

The War Department trials caused some great strides to be made in vehicle design, more for robustness and reliability than for productivity, but a reliable vehicle which rarely breaks down and requires less servicing also requires less 'spare' cover in the fleet and so is, in itself, an aid to increased productivity. Examples of some of the developments brought about either directly or indirectly by the WD trials were a move away from wood to either cast-spoked or dished steel wheels and an increased use of all-gear transmission in place of chain drive – although chains with all their attendant problems of equalizing left-side and right-side tension, continued for a while with some manufacturers and in some weight categories.

Mention has just been made of servicing, which we tend to forget was such a major feature of vehicle operation. In Hemingway's *Farewell to Arms* there is a description of field ambulances returning from duty in filthy weather, with exhausted drivers having to carry out their oil changes before going off duty! In civilian operations, too, part of the day was spent on servicing and repairs as a matter of routine.

The First World War itself gave motorized transport an even greater impetus, one it badly needed to make designers, manufacturers and operators alike realize the potential that was there to be exploited. Development, then, whether for productivity reasons or for reliability and robustness, had not been in vain and it is said that it was in the mud of France that the lorry really proved its worth to the general public. Even so, the difficulties faced by civilian operators, including brewers, during the war period should not be forgotten. Any motor vehicles worth having had been commandeered for the war effort and for those which were available, petrol was very scarce. Horses were in very short supply, many thousands having been recruited to the Army Remount Department and, of course, fodder and bedding were supplied to the front as a priority. So, whilst internal

Right: This 2½-tonner was produced by Halley's Industrial Motors of Glasgow in about 1914. Photographed 'for the record' before it was registered or delivered to Smithers Brewery of Brighton, Halley's must have been very pleased with a sale so far south as most of their clientele was from north of the border. The general design is typical of many makes of the period, probably because of the requirements of the War Office subsidy scheme. This vehicle would have been fitted with a Halley engine but, until only a few years previously, Tyler engines would have been the norm. The Halley was a considerably more advanced engine having dual magnetos and a coil and battery ignition system.

George Halley was a brilliant young engineer with a track record of experimentation and innovation on steam vehicles, having founded the Glasgow Motor Lorry Co Ltd in 1901. This company was reformed and renamed in 1906, becoming Halley's Industrial Motors, to concentrate on internal combustion-engined vehicles. In 1927 Halley's were again renamed, as Halley Motors Ltd. They ceased production altogether in 1935, going into liquidation and being acquired by Albion Motors, whose factory they had adjoined in the very early days.

The brass plate clearly shows this to be a Dennis engine but it is, in fact, an early example of badge engineering. White & Poppe, of Coventry, supplied the engines for most of Dennis' commercial vehicles until 1909 when they became the standard fitment. In 1919 Dennis acquired the company and transferred all the production to Guildford. The photo shows the 'T' head engine which was used for many years until eventually replaced by Dennis' own design which used an 'L' head with pushrods.

The name Commer was an abbreviation of the word 'commercial' and early vehicles were badged as 'Commer Car'. Whilst outwardly differing little from contemporary subsidy types, Commers did not meet the War Office requirements although they were widely used for other, non-combatant duties during the war.

The RC model shown won a silver medal in the RAC Commercial Vehicle Trials of 1907 and went on to become the mainstay of Commer's production for over 20 years. By 1907, Commers were being produced at Luton, having previously been based in the Clapham Road in south-west London. They had engines of 32hp with ball-bearings for the crankshaft; final drive was by chains enclosed in an oil-bath.

In 1926 Humber acquired the entire share capital of Commercial Cars Ltd and eventually Commer became a fully-fledged member of the Rootes Group whose advertisements of the time proudly proclaimed: 'Humber – Hillman – Sunbeam-Talbot – Commer – Karrier'. Only the Talbot name survives today, having returned to its birthplace, France, as part of Peugeot-Talbot.

This photograph shows the J-type Thornycroft 3-tonner, earlier models of which were 'subsidy type' vehicles, which qualified for a prewar subsidy from the War Department if the vehicle was kept in a condition which rendered it suitable for commandeering if war broke out. The number-plate tells us that this particular vehicle was registered between October 1917 and October 1922, although it appears to be rather earlier, having solid tyres but electric lighting. The signwriting behind the door illustrates some of the Championship Gold Medals, Prizes and Diplomas won by 'Our Ales and Stout' although all the dates mentioned are prewar. Did they stop giving diplomas – or did they simply stop winning them after the war? Or could this indeed be an earlier vehicle that had done war service and been returned to its operator? The general condition, including the small neat curtains in the rear of the cab, suggest this is unlikely, but it is interesting to conjecture.

On the scuttle can be seen a brass plaque bearing the inscription PERSEVERANCE, the name of one of the redundant horses from this brewery. Today this plaque still adorns a beautifully restored J-type formerly kept at Marlow brewery. Plaques from other redundant horses used to be carried by the modern diesel drays which ran out of Marlow until its closure in 1993.

The Thornycroft J-type had a four-cylinder side-valve engine which developed 40hp at 1,200rpm. Transmission was through a cone clutch and four-speed gearbox to a worm-driven rear axle. This photograph was taken some time after the one shown above and shows at least one slight modification – the horn had been moved to a position under the bonnet, probably to prevent unwanted interference, but also reflecting its conversion to electricity!

Thornycroft, even in 1914, were an old-established firm, with a record of quality and innovation. They had produced steam vehicles of various sorts since the early 1890s and, even then, had drawn upon their experience of building and operating steam launches.

combustion was gaining a foothold, steam still played an important domestic role.

The war also resulted in large numbers of men being trained to drive so when hostilities ceased there was a good supply of drivers, many of them anxious to exploit their newly found driving skills. Yet even if there was work to do, there were not enough vehicles immediately available for them to drive; until, that is, large numbers of ex-WD vehicles – notably Leylands (RAF-type 3-tonners) and Thornycrofts (J-types) – came flooding onto the market as

Registered PB 6272 in Surrey between August 1919 and July 1921, this Belsize operated out of Whitbread's Kingston-upon-Thames depot. The body was almost certainly built locally, probably by E A Turner of Kingston, who would also have done the paintwork. The fact that this appears to be an unimaginative design for 1920 with its archaic scuttle, solid tyres all round and a mixture of acetylene and electric lighting, gives a clue to its being secondhand – possibly even a refurbished wartime vehicle and hence the need for re-registering. It does, though, have shaft-drive transmission to what appears to be quite an up-to-date differential, but is restricted to 12mph, so is probably the 28hp four-cylinder petrol engined 3-tonner. Belsize Motors was a Manchester firm which produced various commercial vehicle types from 1906 until 1918, specializing in fire-fighting vehicles and also offering charabancs. After the First World War they confined their production almost exclusively to light vans and taxicabs, ceasing production altogether in 1925.

secondhand and War Surplus. Many were immediately snapped up by ex-servicemen eager to set themselves up in road transport but, not surprisingly, this large demand, being met by an abundant supply of relatively cheap secondhand vehicles, had a very depressing effect on the new vehicle market – so much so that Leyland Motors set about purchasing every secondhand Leyland they could lay their hands on and refurbishing them at the old Sopwith Aviation Works at Ham, south of London.

The work done by Leyland, and the scale involved, were highly creditable. Far from being a clean-up and repaint, each vehicle was stripped right down, worn or damaged components were replaced and conversions were frequently made from solid to pneumatic tyres and from acetylene to electric lighting. Bodywork, particularly the cab, was generally updated and a very Twenties-looking vehicle emerged from what had been a very Great War design.

Between 1920 and 1940, vehicle development blossomed. Road transport had become an established fact, and operators in general and brewers in particular were again hot on the trail of improved productivity.

The unladen weight of vehicles reduced as engineering became more sophisticated and mathematics was used rather than iron and steel to ensure adequate strength. Payloads increased, mainly as a result of reduced tare weight, since legislation even then was quite firm about what weights could be transmitted to the road by goods vehicles. No-one would deny that the ability of the law-enforcement authorities was less well developed in those days than it is today so observation of the law, too, was decidedly less exact.

Power and speed also made rapid advances although speed was still very restricted – to 12mph for solid-tyred vehicles and to 20mph for most of the others – a limit which was to stay in force until well after the Second World War. Braking systems had to improve in order to handle the higher speeds, gross weights and power, so early mechanisms which relied on rods and cables for their operation gave way to hydraulic, then to vacuum and vacuum-servo systems and, ultimately, to full airbrakes, although the fail-safe systems which are in use today did not arrive until the late Fifties or early Sixties.

Driver comfort and visibility improved, initially by fitting a front windscreen and, later, a roof and eventually

This photograph is from an advertising brochure, being stripped of all its background detail. From the collector's point of view these photos are of less interest as they provide little or no supporting detail. Moreover, the glass plate negative from which this was originally taken has clearly been damaged and there is evidence of 'touching-up'. Nevertheless, there are few pictures of Hallfords on brewery work and we must establish what we can. Hallfords were built at Dartford, in Kent, between 1907 and 1925 and the vehicle illustrated, being a 3 to 4-tonner, probably dates from around 1919. During the war, Hallford concentrated on building chassis only, using engines bought in from Dormans or from White and Poppe. After the war they returned to using their own engines with the 4.9-litre, 32hp model EA which had four cylinders, cast as two pairs. The vehicle had a four-speed transmission and, common throughout the Hallford range, chain drive.

The model designation GH4 on this Leyland indicates that the vehicle is a G-type 4-tonner with the long-frame option. The suffix 'H' was added to indicate that a larger engine had been fitted – 48hp instead of 40hp – and pneumatic tyres. This model was built in its own right from about 1920 but many were, in fact, refurbished and generally updated RAF types from the war.

FN 4466 was registered in Canterbury around 1920, the precise date being difficult to pinpoint since FN registration marks were issued from as early as January 1904 to as late as March 1929.

Two aspects about the photo are worthy of comment; one is the condition of the offside front tyre – which would cause some concern nowadays – and the other is the astonishing amount of beer delivered to one pub at one time. However often did they have deliveries like this?

There was a time when vehicles were built to last – and last. These two pictures, which were taken nearly 50 years apart, show what are basically identical vehicles. OL 1728 appears much as it would have done when first delivered from Daimlers in 1923 even though being a 1920 model the design is beginning to show its age. Daimlers were certainly producing pneumatic-tyred vehicles by 1923 and, in fact, their Series CJ and CK 2 to 3-tonners were equipped with a built-in tyre pump as an optional extra! Apart from the obvious advantages of pneumatic compared with solid tyres, legislation permitted pneumatic-shod vehicles to operate at 30mph whilst the solids were restricted to 12mph – an example of how legislation can affect design trends.

PW 104, originally registered in Norfolk around 1923, has clearly been subjected to updating and other modification, retaining its acetylene lamps but sporting pneumatic tyres on dished wheels rather than the original cast versions. The vehicle in the photograph is a restoration and is seen here on Madeira Drive, Brighton, having completed the Historic Commercial Vehicle Society's annual London to Brighton run, which takes place each year on the first Sunday in May. In its heyday, London to Brighton would have been a marathon-style journey because of the maximum 12mph speed limit.

By 1923 Daimler were already old-established commercial vehicle producers, the first dating back to 1896 although they did not really operate in this country until 1897.

This photo shows a reworked subsidy-type Dennis 4-tonner which was put into service on November 22, 1926 having previously seen service in Surrey where the vehicle was built. The body was also made, fitted and painted in Surrey, by Turners of Kingston.

Concessions to its civilian role, as distinct from its military-subsidy design, were a generally improved cab – the original was a canvas canopy with very little headroom – and closer fitting wings for road rather than cross-country use. It seems strange that such narrow wheels could have had any cross-country ability, but often their narrowness cut through the wet mud on the surface and, presenting very little rolling resistance, ran on the firmer ground beneath.

Between 1909 and 1914, Dennis advertised that they supplied vehicles to several brewers including Arnold Perrett of Gloucester; Fremlin Bros of Maidstone; Gateside Brewery of Newcastle; Hancocks of Cardiff and, of course, as illustrated, Whitbread's of London. Dennis proudly proclaimed that these were 'not only users BUT ACTUAL PURCHASERS'.

doors and side screens as well. To squeeze even more productivity out of the vehicles, experiments were made with lower deck-heights to enable the draymen to handle the loads more easily and with less strain – hence more quickly and for longer periods!

The whole inter-war period was one of innovation, experiment and development with some ideas being successful and going on to become commonplace, and others being markedly less successful and eventually falling by the wayside. Perhaps the most striking and exciting example of the successful is the adoption for road transport of heavy-oil, or diesel engines which were developed for road transport work during the Twenties by the German firm of Maschinenfabrik Augsburg-Nurnberg Aktiengesellschaft for whom Dr Rudolph Diesel worked. Diesels became popular very quickly and were tried for all sorts of applications apart from road transport. The obvious roles, of course, were for stationary engines of various sorts and for marine and rail use, but who would have thought that diesel engines would have found an application in aviation, where they were used to power such aircraft as flying boats, the R101 airship and the Junkers Jumo 205?

Less successful was the brief sortie into electric vehicles, which were little used by brewers and then only for very short-haul work and deliveries close to the brewery. Electrics did catch on to a limited extent in some other delivery roles, Harrods even developing and building their own electrics, but the main area for success with electrically powered vehicles was with floats for bread, milk and even coal delivery. The main objection to electric vehicles was their high unladen weight and their relatively small payload. The majority of the weight of a laden electric vehicle is accounted for by the batteries; that was the case in the

Twenties and Thirties and is still much the case today.

By the end of the Thirties, the options available to a vehicle operator must have been quite bewildering. Horses were still in common use, especially for house-to-house deliveries and for parcels collection and delivery. Steam lorries for the most part had stopped being produced, at least for home use, although those that were still around were quite sophisticated and very quiet. Had they been allowed to, laden steam lorries could easily accelerate, almost silently, up to 50mph. Most manufacturers offered both petrol and diesel options and those which did not could fairly readily be converted – a common practice with bus operators. You could almost have as many axles as you wanted – or were prepared to pay for – but four seems to have been the effective maximum if trailer axles are not counted. Trailers themselves could be articulated, or drawbar or even a combination of both – an intriguing development by Pagefield of which there is no record of brewery use.

The battle had not yet been won between normal control, where the engine was ahead of the driver, under a bonnet, making access for servicing and repairs easier, and forward control, where the engine – usually not muffled for noise or heat in those days – was in the cab with the driver, thus allowing more load-deck space within a given length. Needless to say, there were half-way options, too, such as the semi-forward-control layout with the engine half in and half out of the cab. There was yet another configuration, the proper name for which does not appear to be recorded, but which was commonly known as 'the pig', where most of the engine was ahead of the front axle. Clearly, if there had been a 'right' answer, every operator would have had similar vehicles, and it is fascinating to see the lengths to which

For various reasons electric vehicles did not catch on to any great extent with brewers even though some flirted with the idea for a while. This photograph eloquently illustrates the point about the wide choice of transport mode as it shows horses, steam and motor waggons as well as electric. They were not popular because of their restricted range and because much of their gross weight was taken up with the weight of the batteries, thus restricting payload. This is still much the case over half a century later.

Taken in the Twenties, this photograph shows a typical 'electric' emerging from the North Yard of Whitbread's brewery in Chiswell Street, London – near to where the Barbican is now. In the left foreground is The Brewer's House and behind it are the offices which, in the Eighties were used by the Group Transport and Distribution departments, even though by then no active distribution took place from that site. At the far end can be seen the sundial, and the offices behind this are those which were fire-damaged in 1982.

Body Built & Designed by
E. A. Turner.
163-165 London Road.
Kingston on Thames.

It has already been seen that Dennis were major suppliers to the brewery trade – and not just to Whitbread's. Their vehicles were simple and straightforward – not to say crude in respect of noise insulation and driver comfort! However, they were liked by the operators for their robustness, sound engineering and good service record.

Fleet No 18 was a 6-tonner which entered service at Chiswick Bottling Depot on January 16, 1931. The bodywork is well suited to its task of carrying crated beers, being strong but lightweight. It is likely that, especially in fair weather, the tarpaulin sheet would have been dispensed with as it would have slowed down both loading and turn-round times. When not in use it would have been neatly furled atop the cab. Note the odd mixture – especially for the Thirties – of acetylene and electric lighting.

Bedford were also major suppliers to the brewery trade up to the time that they ceased production as Bedfords, a span of nearly 50 years. Bedford started in Britain in 1931 with imported, and rebadged, Buick chassis. Offering a robust, tried and proven engine of 27 RAC horsepower at a realistic price, they soon caught on with all sorts of operators, building up an immense and popular following, including a club for Bedford drivers.

The photograph shows a publicity shot of a WTL of 1934–5 vintage. This attractive petrol-powered 3-tonner continued in production, with only minor style detail modifications, such as the radiator grille (but not surround) which was changed from mesh to narrow vertical bars. The example shown is a publicity vehicle – hence the lack of proper livery – and features chrome-plating where the standard version would normally have been painted.

The chain-and-stake body is of interest; this later developed to become the 'boxing-ring' dray body whose name is self-explanatory.

46

Leyland supplied vehicles to the brewery trade for many years and even published a booklet in the Fifties entitled 'Leylands for the Brewer'. They were particularly active at the heavier end of the weight range as instanced by this Leyland Hippo, which operated from Whitbread's Chiswick Bottling Depot from August 23, 1934. Registered BPJ 772 with Fleet No 263, this 12-tonner would have carried beers brewed at the London breweries and bottled at Chiswick to other distribution depots around London.

This unusually long wheelbase reflects the fact that, compared with bulk or cask beers, crates were quite light in weight and, to obtain the maximum productivity from the vehicle, wheelbases had to be extended. There was, of course, a practical limit to how high the crates could be stacked so there was no other effective way to put the load on. Even so, with the front axle set so far forward, the rear bogie so far back and no power-assistance to the steering, this must have been a heavy vehicle to drive.

Whilst not a dray, this attractive 1934 example of a commercial-bodied Ford Model Y illustrates the increasing use by breweries of specialized vehicles. The model shown is a local retail delivery van, which would have delivered made-up orders to customers in the area. This enabled orders which were of a reasonable size to be made direct to customers without tying up the expensive resources involved in sending a dray. In this case the retailer is simply the off-sales department of the 'tied' pub next door, the Robin Hood at Dagenham. The term 'tied' means that the pub is not free to buy its beer where it pleases, being tied to the brewery and hence only being permitted to sell their products.

The saloon version of the Model Y had its price slashed in 1935 to make it the first £100 car. Popularly known as 'the £100 Ford', it fulfilled part of Henry Ford's dream of providing motor cars for the masses.

A lovely working shot of a Bedford long-wheelbase 3-tonner, model WTL, delivering J W Green's 'Noted Luton Ales' to The Fox public house in Luton around 1934. There are several points of interest in this picture which can be compared with the earliest of horse-drawn drays. Unloading is, as was fairly conventional, over the tailboard, using the barrel-skid hooked into the top of the hinged tailboard.

The body sides are strong but not solid to avoid excessive weight and at the front end of the load platform is a steel rod, supported in the middle, into which the barrel-skid could be hooked to facilitate side-unloading – which would have been desirable on a vehicle with such a long platform. The drayman (driver) is on the vehicle and the trouncer, who has the heaviest part of the task, guides the cask to the ground whence it is rolled into position.

The cellar flap is not visible in the picture so it can be surmised that unloading will be completed before moving the casks to the flap for lowering into the underground cellar. Note that the billycock hats have been replaced by peaked caps but that the leather apron remains.

For many years Dennis were major suppliers to the brewery trade. This 4-tonner of 1935 vintage was registered in Surrey and clearly shows the distinctive Dennis radiator shape, bearing the legend on its grille 'BEER IS BEST' which was also used by several other brewers. It is seen here emerging from the Guildford depot of Friary Meux, so it is in every sense a local vehicle, made, registered and used in Guildford. The year 1935 was the first in which Dennis offered a diesel-engine option and the first was fitted in a Dennis Lancet II passenger chassis. Early Dennis diesels were of the Lanova type but, later, Dennis O-types were fitted. CPJ 771 is almost certainly petrol-engined.

Saurer was a make which was not widely used by brewers and may only have been used by Whitbread's because of their strong links with the continent. However, from as early as 1928 Saurer were among the first to offer diesel engines with options of four- or six-cylinder petrol or diesel engines, so it is quite possible that this splendid dray from the early Thirties was fitted with a diesel engine for trials in the brewery's delivery fleet. Certainly, many more were ordered by this particular brewer, so there must have been some commercial advantage in using them.

Note the 'C' licence disc in the windscreen. This system was in use up to the 1968 Transport Act – Barbara Castle's 'magnum opus' which transformed the British road transport industry almost as much as had nationalization some 20 years previously. 'C' licences authorized the holder to deliver his own goods only and was restricted to a radius of 30 miles from the operating centre.

development went to provide the right productivity solution to different productivity questions.

By 1938, Europe was again girding her loins for war and, whilst vehicle development continued, it was, as in the pre-First World War period, mainly for military purposes. As a result, civilian development stagnated until after 1945. Indeed, in the early Forties, the problem for many operators was to obtain any vehicles at all with another World War rapidly developing.

Breweries, however, may have enjoyed a small dispensation in this respect. When Brickwood's brewery, in Portsmouth, was bombed – so the story goes – it was considered to have such strategic importance as a means of producing a vital ingredient for the relaxation of naval crews returning to their home port that it was permitted to have priority for war damage repairs.

Interestingly, with the shortage of conventional materials for constructing fermentation vessels – normally made of copper – an experiment was tried with vessels lined with top-quality bitumen. This proved to be amazingly successful and some of the bitumen-lined vats were still in use in the early Eighties! Similar dispensations may have been available for vehicles, but it seems unlikely that applications would have been accepted other than at places of some strategic importance.

This vehicle, registered in London around 1937, is from the Scottish truck-builder Albion, who operated out of Scotstoun, Glasgow, from 1903 until 1972, when they were phased out by Leyland. In fact Albion was founded a year earlier in 1902, at Finniestoun, Glasgow, where they produced their first commercial vehicle which was a simple affair having a little two-cylinder 8hp engine and tiller steering. After 1972 the plant was used by Leyland for some years for the production of components, mainly axles. By the Thirties Albion were a force to be reckoned with, producing lightweight vehicles which were of fairly basic design but could take maximum advantage of the regulations relating to unladen weight and speed. The vehicle shown is probably the 5½-tonner, model 127, but it is difficult to be certain with such a square end-on view. The model 127 weighed in at under 2 tons unladen and so could operate at 30mph, making it extremely popular with some operators. Albion, whilst noted for the quality of their product, could rarely claim to be at the forefront of fashion with their designs, the basic design in the photo remaining fairly well unchanged right up to the Fifties. Albion acquired Halley Industrial Motors in 1935 and were themselves acquired by Leyland Motors in 1951.

Mammoth Major – one of the many names used by AEC having the same initial letter and known as the M-family. Others were Mandator, Marshal, Mercury, Monarch and, after the acquisition of Maudslay Motors, Mogul, Majestic, Mustang and Militant; AEC used R-family names for their buses. The model shown is a Mammoth Major Mark II, type 680, registered in August 1937 in Surrey. This 15-ton GVW (gross vehicle weight) eight-wheeler was in production from 1933 until 1947, and was available with the AEC six-cylinder, 7,581cc diesel engine of 95 to 105bhp. The vehicle shown, Fleet No 333, had a ventilating trap fitted to the cab – a feature considered sufficiently noteworthy to be recorded on the back of the photo! Widely used by the brewing trade both for long-haul domestic work and for those who had overseas operations, for export transfers, this was a good-looking and reliable motor which was liked by its drivers. Even by the standards of the day, it was a fairly noisy vehicle to drive, but the engine sound had a smoothness which some of its competitors lacked. AEC acquired a number of other producers over the years, including Hardy Motors, which for several years had used AEC components; both Crossley and Maudslay were acquired in 1948 with two bodybuilding firms, Park Royal and Chas H Roe, following in 1949. The year 1962 saw the addition of Thornycroft and the merger of the newly named company – Associated Commercial Vehicles – with their old rival Leyland. By 1980 the name AEC no longer appeared on any new vehicles. Fortunately there are several in preservation ranging from eight-wheeled flatbeds and tankers to the smaller dropside and tipper vehicles which AEC also produced.

This Chevrolet Model 40/60 50cwt (2½ tons payload) was intended for experimental use to assess its performance against the equivalent offering from Bedford, even though they were both from the GMC stable. It may also have been all that was available as Bedford were suddenly very busy producing vehicles for the war effort, war having been declared just two months before this vehicle went into service in November 1939. The vehicle is in fact dressed out for wartime operations with hooded headlamps and the bumper and wings painted white for improved visibility in the blackout. Fleet No 410, with its smooth-running six-cylinder OHV engine, was registered in London but ended up working out of Plymouth depot. Chevrolet trucks in this weight range sold well during the Thirties with nearly 120,000 sold in 1930 – just behind Ford's total. In 1933 and 1934, they outsold Fords, but lost the lead again in 1935. After the outbreak of war few more were sold in this country and, by the time the war was over, Bedford reigned supreme.

CHAPTER FOUR

Maturity

The postwar years up to about 1960 are often referred to as the 'golden years' of road haulage. The British commercial vehicle industry was the strongest in the world, helped by the massive postwar export drive and a tame colonial market which had been starved of vehicles for over six years. In those days there was still a wide choice of British lorry manufacturers from which to select and foreign competition was considered to be more of a novelty than a threat.

Even though in the Forties and for some years to come the heavier vehicles had to operate at 20mph, large amounts of goods traffic travelled by road, demonstrating just how flexible and efficient road transport is in a small island like Britain compared with other modes of transport. Relatively small payloads and slow running speeds are quickly compensated for by the advantages of being able to run journeys from door-to-door at whatever time is convenient to the consignor and consignee, without having to load and unload on to other types of waggon. Then, as now, goods transport by road represented a reasonable bargain for most categories of traffic – and until the Sixties there was no motorway network worth its name to make it as effective as it is today.

After 1947, which saw the nationalization of nearly all the haulage fleets of any consequence, the scene may have been less colourful: British Road Services vehicles were either red for haulage, or green for parcels – but it was certainly no less interesting. There were still many 'own-account' operators and all of these had their own liveries which were often very distinctive and could be identified by the enthusiast at considerable distances on the road.

Brewers were probably the largest group of own-account operators, the majority of their fleet being dedicated to delivering to pubs. Moves towards the huge brewing conglomerates of today, in which the different processes are concentrated at one location, necessitating much trunk movement of part-processed product, had not yet started,

and brewing, bottling, retailing and consuming all took place within relatively few miles of the brewery. Most brewery vehicles, though, were not particularly colourful, with dark blues, dark greens and browns seeming to predominate, but almost invariably they were well-kept, with shining paintwork and, if there was any, brasswork. Some brewers were known to use real gold-leaf for the lettering on their vehicles, this being supplied to the bodybuilders or painters in exactly the right quantities! Other fleets used the brass plates, formerly worn by their horses and bearing their names, on their vehicles so that there was something to polish!

Immediately after the war, vehicles were in very short supply; where production was available, preference, often reluctantly, was given to export sales to try to put the country back on its feet, and many operators had to make do with elderly and already hard-worked lorries, including war surplus vehicles when they became available. These were sometimes re-engined more than once during their lifetime and, if one was available, the opportunity was often taken to fit a diesel engine, several proprietary makes being available, with Meadows and Gardner seeming to be most popular. Fitting, of course, was done by the operators themselves who usually had in-house workshops and undertook tasks on an everyday basis which would undoubtedly require specialist attention today.

Gardner acquired the nickname 'the *legendary* Gardner' by virtue of its rugged, day-in, day-out reliability. Gardners were never the most exciting performers amongst the diesel engine fraternity, but for sheer quality of engineering they were difficult to beat. It was relatively commonplace to hear of Gardners running for a million miles without major overhaul – something which would be unlikely today with vehicle replacement intervals of around seven years at the most. It is perhaps not surprising that fairground operators and showmen use Gardners almost exclusively for their

One manufacturer which was little represented in brewery fleets before the war was Bedford. Having started in this country in 1931 as 'GM's British Commercial' and originally badged as Chevrolets, Bedfords went on to enjoy, by the Sixties, the major market share for brewery transport – and for most other distribution tasks, too. Possibly their postwar popularity was connected with the fact that so many ex-serviceman had experience and good reports of the marque, Bedford having produced some quarter of a million lorries for the armed forces, in addition to tanks, jerrycans, steel helmets and many other accoutrements of war. Amongst the earliest models available after the war were the OS and OL-types. These were available both as 2 to 3-tonners and 5-tonners in short or long-wheelbase form, and the picture shows the long-wheelbase 5-tonner. These were, in fact, also produced before the war, but production was interrupted by the war effort in 1940. It resumed in 1945 and ran through to 1952 when the model was superseded by the S-type, (the civilian version of the slightly later military R-type, and commonly known as the 'Big Bedford'). The O-types were fitted with the standard Bedford petrol-powered 28hp engine, with its very characteristic sound. The photograph shows a line-up of some of the very first of this model to be available, taken just before the war at Ind Coope and Allsopp's brewery, which was on the site of the later Romford Brewery.

Seddon produced vehicles for brewers at both the heavy and light ends of the vehicle spectrum. An elderly example of a 6-tonner, meaning 6-tons payload and probably nearly 10 tons all-up, is this 1943 forward-control Model 6T supplied to the Isle of Wight brewers Mew Langton. The circle-encrusted diamond on the radiator grille indicates that a Perkins diesel engine is fitted and, in fact, this one was fitted with a P6. This model was introduced in 1939 and earlier versions had a chrome-plated radiator – this one has been painted – and six-stud wheels which were later replaced, as on this example, by the more conventional eight studs. The body looks like a home-made affair, converting a flat platform vehicle, suitable only for cased beer, to a more general purpose – from the brewer's point of view – stake-sided type.

vehicle-mounted mobile generating sets and for many years there was a good export trade in used Gardner engines to China for use in junks, a trade shared with AEC.

Just after the war, as already mentioned, horses were still in wide use; steam was becoming rather less common and was seen mainly for local heavy work, especially around the docks, and for road-mending and tar-spraying, one surviving in this role into the Eighties. Vehicles which had been converted during the war to run on producer gas were converted back again and the technology seems to have died. Producer gas engines worked by heating coal or other fuels so as to give off a combustible gas – much like a

A delightful street-scene taken in late 1946 or early 1947 which clearly illustrates the diversity of transport available at the time. The main vehicle in the photo is the Dennis 5-tonner, a vehicle much-liked by brewers. Of equal interest is the covered horse-drawn waggon with its poster proclaiming the disadvantages and dangers of public ownership of transport. It reads: 'DANGER. Stop Nationalisation of Transport' and continues with a message exhorting the public to involve their MPs. History records the fact that the opposition failed, with the result that British Road Services was formed. In the background, weaving its way amongst the traffic, is a prewar Albion boxvan from the fleet of W Young and Sons and parked either side of it are an AEC Mammoth Major tanker and an ex-military Bedford OY.

mobile town-gasworks – which then powered a suitably modified conventional engine. This was used to a reasonable extent by bus companies, but not very much by brewers as the loss of performance rendered them unsuitable for large loads or for hilly areas.

As vehicle production slowly became available to the home market, favoured makes began to emerge amongst the brewers, and names like AEC, Dennis, Leyland, Seddon and even Albion began to predominate. Several years were to pass before brewers' delivery vehicles became almost exclusively Bedfords, Commers and Fords. On the transfer, or trunk side of the business, there was as much variety then as at any time before or since.

So perhaps there was more variety than choice, some of it being provided by ingenious conversions of nominally unsuitable vehicles for a new role. Many ideas were already on offer from manufacturers, ranging from the three-wheeled 'mechanical horses' made by Scammell and Karrier, through normal and forward-control four-wheelers

to the mostly forward-control six, Chinese-six and eight-wheelers.

Chapter 2 showed that one way of squeezing more payload onto vehicles was to add axles, and there were various ways of doing this, either by doubling-up at the back, or the front, or both. Adding a single undriven axle at the back was the simplest way and many conversions of this type were made, not so much by brewers, but quite often in haulage fleets. The modern-day equivalent of such a conversion (ignoring technicalities like braking systems, suspension, engine, transmission and chassis ratings!) would be to convert from 16 or 17 tonnes gross vehicle weight (GVW – ie the weight of the vehicle and its load) to 20 or 21 tonnes. The 1991 maximum gross vehicle weight permissible on three axles was 24 tonnes but these uprated conversions could not become a full 24-tonne outfit because of restrictions on their maximum permissible train weight. Most 17-tonners have a maximum permissible GTW of 21 or 22 tons, hence the limit on the GVW of the conversion!

This very early Bedford, the model WLG 2-ton, long wheelbase dropside lorry was produced from 1931 until the outbreak of war, being replaced – for a year only, as production turned to military types – by the model ML in 1939. This example, photographed in 1934 whilst unloading in Bristol (with the aid of a barrel-skid), was owned and operated by Mr Robert Hobbs, on contract to Coate's Cider. The WLG, and its short wheelbase counterparts, the WH and WHG, were the forerunners of what became the best-known, and probably the best-loved of British commercials – whose advertising slogan was 'Bedford – you see them everywhere!'

Apart form uprating to 28hp just before the war and the introduction of an 'extra duty' version, in the Fifties, Bedford's 27hp petrol engine remained virtually unchanged until the company's demise in the late Eighties. In common with the SS Jaguar, which was introduced the same year, the unit was a six-cylinder, in-line engine of 3½ litres capacity and both offered 'lots of torque and rugged ability at a reasonable price'. These engines were produced in their tens of thousands and many are still running today – even spares are hardly any problem.

The addition of the extra axle at the front gives the Chinese-six configuration, which has already been mentioned, and it may be of interest to consider this axle configuration more closely as its use has waxed and waned in the brewery industry right up to the present day.

The Chinese-six is a six-wheeled vehicle, but it is unusual in having two axles at the front instead of at the back. Both of the front axles were required to steer, and some clever engineering and complicated steering geometry was needed to make this viable: lines drawn through the hubs at right angles to the direction of each individual wheel all pass through the same point – the centre of the vehicle's turning circle. If this does not sound complicated, try sketching it and then work out how it's done with steel! I can recall as a youngster seeing a Chinese-six in a lay-by on the old A1 Great North Road, with a broken steering arm and with all the wheels on the two front axles pointing in different directions. I have often wondered how they managed to get it into the lay-by!

So, if it was difficult to design and build, why did anyone bother with it? The answer lies in the vagaries of British transport legislation, which sometimes seems to operate to everyone's disadvantage.

A vehicle could be loaded at the depot up to its legal maximum and then, after making a delivery and actually removing weight from the vehicle, it could become illegally overloaded. This is because the law does not just lay down limits on the total weight, but also on the weight which can be transmitted to the road by each axle. As explained in Chapter 2, on a four-wheeled vehicle, the load behind the rear axle acts as a counterbalance to the weight on the front axle. If this load is removed, the counterbalance is destroyed

and the front axle becomes illegal. Placing an additional axle at the front helped overcome this problem.

Two front axles, however, introduced other problems: steering lock on Chinese-sixes and eight-leggers was never very good and, with old-fashioned suspensions, they were exceedingly uncomfortable to drive anywhere where there were bumps. Just as you were on your way down from the front axle hitting the bump, you would receive another jar as the second axle hit it. There were even some cases of permanent damage to drivers' and trouncers' backs from this problem – which is why they faded out until suspensions improved. However, the problem was particularly acute on the three-axled vehicle, perhaps because the four-axled variety was that much heavier and thus less frisky, tending to lumber over the bumps rather than bounce over them.

Conversion to the Chinese-six format did not give such a large increase in payload as conversion to a conventional six, because steered axles cannot, by law, carry the same weight as unsteered axles. (Incidentally, there is a modern-day exception to this with self-steering axles on some trailers.) The Chinese-six conversion, in the modern-day equivalence just described, increases GVW from 17 tonnes to a maximum of about 22 tonnes depending upon technical factors. Adding an additional axle at both ends was usually beyond what was reasonable as a conversion and, if any conversions were carried out it is likely that it would be from Chinese-six to eight-legger. The so-called eight-legger nowadays has a maximum GVW of 30 tons, around 20 of which are payload.

Other useful ways to gain payload included pulling trailers, and this is discussed in the next chapter.

Rather larger than Dennis' Max and Pax models was the Jubilant. The vehicle shown may have had an interesting history although, over time, records have become confused and it is not always possible to relate with certainty a set of records to a particular vehicle. HYU 914 was a fairly early example of Dennis' forward-control offerings in this form, dating from 1947, being the year in which it first entered service on October 6. At this time, records suggest, it may have had a petrol engine – the Dennis four-cylinder side-valve unit – although if it did, it must have been somewhat underpowered with a 12-ton payload.

However, it seems that in March 1954 it was converted to a Perkins P6 diesel, even though the more usual engine for the Jubilant was Dennis' own 'O6' 8-litre unit. The O6 engine suffered heavy oil consumption, though, and was exceptionally noisy (even for a Dennis engine!) when warm, partly due to all the gears being at the back of the engine. The usual gearbox for the Jubilant was a five-speed 'crash' box, with 5th gear being an overdrive. The chassis and cab were (obviously) provided by Dennis Bros of Guildford and the body – or at least one of the bodies during its lifetime – was by Sparshatts. It appears that this particular vehicle had a number of bodies over the years since no less than three sets of dimensions exist for it! This suggests that apart from its normal working duties it may have been used for development work. The body illustrated is described both as being 24ft and 23ft 6in long, and as 7ft 4in and 7ft 6in wide 'with normal sides'. Another set of dimensions is given as 22ft 6in long, 7ft 8in high, 7ft 6in wide with a platform height of 3ft 11in, which seems very low for this type of vehicle.

Not uncommon amongst drays of the period were Albions. Produced in Scotland and, many years later, being absorbed into the huge Leyland empire, Albions were popular for their robustness, simplicity, quality of build and reliability. Their emblem, the rising sun, was accompanied by the slogan: 'Sure as Sunrise'. This photo shows an Albion CX3L fitted with the maker's own diesel engine (the four-cylinder, 75bhp, model EN286), which entered service in April 1947. The body type is known as a 'boxing-ring' for fairly obvious reasons, and this name stuck until recent times when the type was discontinued. With a platform height of 4ft 1in, this would not have been an easy vehicle on which to work the load and, with 7 tons carried on its 19ft 9in by 7ft 2in body, added to its 4 ton 18cwt unladen weight and no power-steering, it probably wasn't all that easy to drive, either!

Dennis, as already seen, was a major supplier of vehicles to breweries for many years and during the Forties, Fifties and even on into the Sixties, their product range developed in line with the needs of the brewers. At the beginning of the period their range was characterized by the bonneted or normal-control Dennis Pax, and various experiments were tried on this chassis, including adding axles and lowering the deck-height to assist with unloading mainly cased beers, but also – and perhaps to a greater extent as time went on – beer in casks. The vehicle illustrated, fleet number D65 ('D' for Dennis – a characteristic of Whitbread's fleet numbering right up to the mid-Eighties), was registered in late 1948 in London for use on deliveries of bottled Mackeson Stout. Many of the Mackeson vehicles were liveried in black and white, but this diesel-engined model is wearing the tan shade of brown with black mudguards and wings which Whitbread used on some occasions.

A scene from Whitbread's Chiswell Street North Yard in 1948. Vehicles D1, D4 and D12 are new into the fleet (and are sisters of the one in the photo on page 53). Also in the yard are three 'electrics' – note the Whitbread numbering, 'E' for Electric rather than, for example, 'W' for Walker, who seems the likely manufacturer. At the end of the yard is an earlier Saurer, a make widely used by Whitbread in its Brussels operation. The one in the picture, though, has conventional right-hand drive so may just be an oddity on trial in the home fleet.

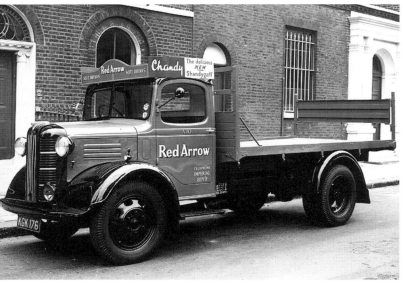

So successful was the Bedford O-type (page 52) that it was copied, more or less blatantly, by other manufacturers. No copy appeared more blatant than Austin's who strenuously denied copying anything, probably quite rightly as both were introduced to the market almost simultaneously. The Austin had a three-man, all-steel cab, as had the Bedford, as well as an overhead-valve engine and hydraulic brakes, features which did not filter through to their cars until after the war. Illustrated is the 2 to 3-tonner which, much to Austin's chagrin, was always known as 'the Birmingham Bedford'. The example shown was registered in early 1949 in London and was engaged almost exclusively on soft drinks deliveries to pubs and corner shops.

By comparison with the CX3L, this Albion FT3L, which followed only 18 months later, in November 1948, looks altogether more modern. Chassis dumbirons are virtually enclosed; headlights look as if they were meant to be there rather than being fitted as an afterthought, and the cab is somehow much more stylish, even though the older vehicle does have more of a nostalgic, functional beauty about it! KMM 122 is only a 6-tonner, compared with LKJ's 7 tons but of considerable interest is the improvement made in the gross:tare ratio. LKJ grossed (ie weighed, all-up) 12,116kg (of which 4,989kg was the unladen weight and the payload was 7,127kg), thus the gross:tare ratio is 2.43:1. The newer vehicle, whilst only carrying 6,109kg, did so with a tare of 2,994kg, grossing 9,103kg, a ratio of 3.29:1, providing an eloquent testimony to what can be achieved by persistent effort.

Body dimensions for the FT3L were 17ft by 6ft 10in with 2in saved on the platform height, which was down to 3ft 11in.

For many of Whitbread's 'transfer' operations, the preferred vehicle for many years was the AEC Mammoth Major, which could have been seen in Whitbread colours right through from the Mark I to the Mark V versions. For some reason, brewers rarely refer to 'trunking' for long-distance work, instead preferring to talk about 'transfer' – usually from brewery to bottling plant or from bottling plant to distribution depot. NGF 403 was a flat-platform *conversion*, although from what it was converted is not recorded. Its body length was 24ft within an overall length of 30ft 2in and its body/overall width was 7ft 6in. Platform height is recorded as an amazing 3ft 8in, but this must be the laden height since the photo suggests it is running on 40in tyres, and approximate scaling indicates an unladen deck-height of well over 4ft. One wonders who the records were designed to impress!

COMPARE *these* OPERATING COSTS

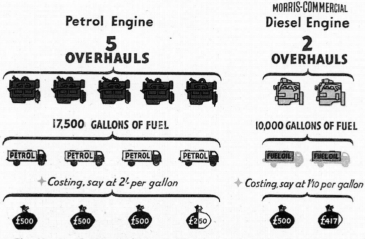

200,000 MILES

Petrol Engine
5
OVERHAULS

MORRIS-COMMERCIAL
Diesel Engine
2
OVERHAULS

17,500 GALLONS OF FUEL

10,000 GALLONS OF FUEL

Costing, say at 2¹ per gallon

Costing, say at 1¹⁰ per gallon

£500 £500 £500 £250

£500 £417

The Morris-Commercial Diesel about halves fuel bills and spends less time off the road.

Approximate costs have been used as price of fuel fluctuates

The diesel engine wins, because oil costs less than petrol and because a diesel engine does more miles to the gallon, for it is a great top-gear performer. Gears are used less; a higher average speed is maintained. Overall fuel costs are almost halved. Moreover, less time is spent off the road for maintenance and service. With only two overhauls against the five necessary for a petrol engine over the same period, a diesel-powered vehicle cannot fail to earn bigger profits. And even maintenance between major overhauls is reduced—there is no electrical ignition system, no distributor, no sparking plugs—there are less things that can go wrong or need replacement in a compression ignition engine.

Bearings and working parts are larger, tougher—they have to be in a diesel engine. They last longer. But when a major overhaul is necessary the engine need not be moved from the frame. Another money-saving feature.

By 1950 most manufacturers had caught on to the idea that diesel engines were worth having. Some used proprietary engines, mainly Gardners at the top end of the weight range and Perkins at the bottom end, but there were still many firms offering their own make of engine. Amongst the less common proprietary diesels were those made under licence from the Swiss concern Saurer by Morris Motors and fitted, as an alternative to the 80bhp petrol unit, in their 5-ton, forward-control Morris Commercials. Contemporary sales literature claimed that, 'the Morris Commercial Saurer diesel engine halves costs and slashes maintenance bills because engine life is increased *two and a half times*. With oil as a fuel, cylinder wear is negligible and the engine runs cooler – there is *no* wide range of operating temperatures'. The leaflet goes on to claim that, '*all* the fuel is burnt ... there is *no* waste' and that 'there is *no unburnt fuel* in the exhaust gases'. Extravagant claims indeed, but the fact that claims like this were made indicated that there was considerable interest in economy and, possibly, an – albeit embryonic – appreciation of the environmental advantages of the diesel. This extract from the Morris Commercial brochure of May 1950 indicates, though, just how much education – even of operators – there was to be done.

As well as Dennis, several other vehicle manufacturers were of major importance to the brewers. Amongst these were Leyland who in the early Fifties published a very limited edition of a booklet entitled 'Leylands for the Brewer'. These individually produced brochures, bound in black with the recipient's name gold-tooled on the cover, are a treasured collector's item, being individually typed and with original photographs bound into them. Two of the advertising 'pulls' from this brochure are reproduced here and compared with some present-day advertising are very informative. No approximations here – if the mileage was 101,022 that is how it was recorded, with no rounding to 100,000, and fuel consumption advertised to the second decimal place! However, it does indicate just how seriously productivity was taken by the brewers if it warranted advertisements of this nature being directed specifically towards them.

One of the vehicles featured in Leyland's brewery advertisement was the solo Octopus. Octopus was the animal name given to all eight-wheelers made by Leyland although, later, when such names as AEC, Albion, Guy and others joined the Leyland marque, other model names traditionally associated with eight-leggers were also seen; names such as Mammoth Major, Caledonian, Warrior and, later and more in line with today's number and letter truck model identifications, Guy's Big J8. The term 'solo' simply meant without trailer: trailers were more popular in the Forties and Fifties than they were in the Sixties and Seventies although since then there has been a resurgence in their use, even if not to any great extent in brewery fleets.

The vehicle illustrated was supplied new in 1951 to William Hancock & Co Ltd, and is fitted with an all-metal platform body 24ft 6in long. All-metal bodies were favoured by some brewers because of their ability to withstand the hard wear they received from casks and general usage. This photo illustrates effectively the large carrying capacity of the Octopus.

Possibly one of the most elegant and beautiful vehicles of its era – at least in appearance – was the Maudslay Mogul. Seen here with a 20ft fixed-sided body, 7ft 4in wide, for 7½ to 8-tons payload, this AEC diesel-powered dray was registered in London and probably operated out of Whitbread's Chiswick depot. Although records no longer exist to confirm where MLE 404 operated, it is known to have entered service on December 1, 1951.

For many years Maudslay had used AEC componentry and were eventually acquired by their erstwhile supplier, ultimately becoming part of the giant Leyland Group whence the Maudslay name disappeared. Some of the model names, however, all of which began with the letter M – such as Mustang and Marathon – survived to adorn AECs. It is sad to see how many once-great names disappeared into the maw of Leyland – Albion, AEC, Guy, Maudslay, Scammell, Thornycroft and many others, especially if the names previously absorbed by companies later acquired by Leyland are included.

Also featured in the Fifties' Leyland brewery advertisement was the Steer – a play on words since all Leylands were named after animals (the so-called Leyland zoo) and this is a twin-steer vehicle. It had a gross rating of 15½ tons, of which 10 were payload, and the twin front axles allowed better weight distribution at the front and fewer problems with diminishing loads. The advertisement declares that such a vehicle would have covered 11.36 miles for every gallon of diesel. The vehicle shown was registered in Gloucester in February 1951 and was one of 60 delivered to Ansell's brewery. It had a platform length of 20ft 6in and could carry 245 two-dozen cases of bottled beer, or 24 hogsheads with smaller casks on top, which makes an interesting comparison with man's earliest attempts at productivity!

Showing that superstition can be found in the transport office as much as anywhere else, this Seddon Mark 5L, also pictured on the previous page, entered service in January 1954 as Fleet No 12A. This was a slightly unusual combination in that several companies collaborated to produce the final outfit. Seddon produced the chassis and running gear and carried out the assembly; Perkins provided their 85bhp P6 engine and Express Motor Bodies Ltd provided the cab and assisted Whitbread in producing the body.

It was not uncommon for transport fleets to indulge in a little DIY, especially where bodies were concerned, but for larger fleets this was usually confined to experimental or development types. It is not immediately obvious what is under development here, but the unladen weight of only 3 ton 1cwt 0qr 17lb (3,113kg) may give a clue to the use of light alloys or other weight-saving ideas. The overall length of this handsome vehicle was 21ft 6in and it was, conventionally, 7ft 6in wide.

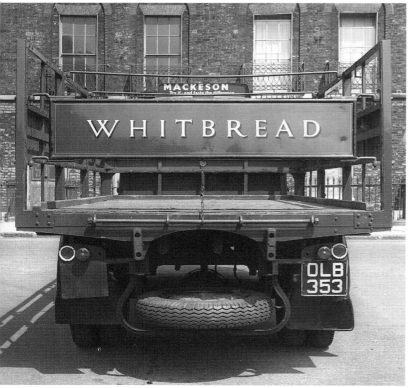

The smallest vehicle ever produced by Seddon was a 25cwt normal-control van, but also very much at the lighter end of Seddon's offerings was this Mark 7L 3-tonner. With a Perkins P4 engine, a cab by Express Motor Bodies and a body made in-house by the operator, Fleet No S12 entered service at Hythe brewery in January 1954. With a low platform height of 3ft 10in possible because of its small wheels, this dray weighed in, unladen, at 2.9.1.24 which is the shorthand for 2 ton 9cwt 1qr 24lb (or 2,518kg). Body dimensions were 14ft in length within an overall length of 19ft 6in, a width of only 7ft 4in and an overall height of 7ft 6in.

Left and right: Also of 3-tons carrying capacity is this much more purposeful-looking Mark 7L with stake-sided body. Entering service on March 18, 1954, this Perkins P4 diesel-engined dray had both cab and body produced by Marshalls of Cambridge. Body dimensions were broadly similar to those in the previous photo, being an inch longer and having 4in extra height and width. The platform height, though, was only 3ft 6in, a worthwhile improvement over the Express Motor Bodies version but, whatever else was gained, payload was lost for the unladen weight had crept back to 2 ton 14cwt (2,749kg), no doubt mainly because of the stake-sided body. Whitbread and Bass for many years were probably the joint leaders in the development of the ideal dray – hence the large amount of photographs and other records which have survived. The twin targets were always low deck-height and low unladen weight and many prototypes and much money was spent in pursuit of this ideal.

Note the doors with hinges at the rear. This was often done where the front edge of the door was curved, so that at least the hinges could lie in the same vertical, straight line. This, together with the front step location, must have called for some nifty footwork to avoid legs becoming tangled on entering the cab!

An interesting comparison with the standard Express Motor Bodies cab is this De Luxe cab fitted on Fleet No S (for Seddon) 18, based at Hythe, in Kent. This Perkins P6-engined, 6-ton Mark 5L, in Mackeson livery, had similar length available as body space; its platform height was 4ft. The fact that the unladen weight has been clearly entered in the records – as well as on the fuel tank – adds further to the hypothesis that experiments were on-going with reductions in the tare weight of drays – this one tipped the scales at a mere 2 ton 19cwt 2qr 18lb (3,037kg).

This photograph is difficult to date accurately since it was taken before the vehicle was registered and so there is no number-plate to go by. However, the mid-Fifties would be a reasonable guess, judged by the Kleer-Vu wrap-around windscreen, pioneered by Boalloy at Congleton, Cheshire, a little further south than Preston, where the Seddons were made.

Left and this page: An example of Dennis' forward-control products is seen in the form of the Dennis Max, RGC 201. Registered in London for use on transfer work to and from Whitbread's depot at Queens Road, Ashton-under-Lyme, this attractive vehicle is a particular favourite with the author, if only because the number-plate consists of his initials! Entering service on July 28, 1955 in the dropside form shown, this diesel-powered vehicle, whose unladen weight was 4 ton 15cwt 2qr and 21lb (4,870kg), had a carrying capacity of 7½ tons and was listed as a Flat Platform *conversion*. The body measured 20ft long and was 7½ft wide. Various experiments were tried with different bodies on this vehicle including an ingenious flat body, dished along the centre-line so that stacks of crated beer leaned towards the centre, thus being more stable and requiring less load-retention.

Left and right: Entering service on September 19, 1957, this handsome Mark V AEC Mammoth Major had a flat-platform body measuring 24ft 6in by 7ft 10in, capable of carrying 15-tons payload. The photo clearly shows the fitting of webbing load restraint gear and the diminutive tailboard which would have been just enough to ensure that the load of beer, in cases, did not start to move relative to the platform – a useful weight-saving idea as, indeed, is the webbing which does away in this instance with the need for body sides. The Mark V followed on directly from the Mark III, a Mark IV never having been produced although some modified Mark IIIs were often, jokingly, referred to as Mark IVs. AEC used to issue very comprehensive maintenance manuals for their vehicles, hard-bound and copiously illustrated with good quality diagrams; so good in fact that they could be used as training manuals. These manuals are now collectors' pieces in their own right.

Thornycroft vehicles were associated with breweries from the early days of motor transport as seen in Chapter 3. These two Glamorgan-registered 5.51-litre diesel Trident 5-tonners were supplied new in April 1957 to E Evans Bevan Ltd of Neath, who provided the famous Vale of Neath ales. By 1957 Thornycroft had started to concentrate their activities in the very much higher weight ranges, producing giant dumptrucks and the magnificent Mighty Antar tank transporter, initially with a petrol engine – the Hercules – but later with a diesel. Thornycroft also produced the Nubian Airfield Rescue Fire Tender and slowly, but surely, supplies of vehicles to brewers dried up.

Left: The Swiftsure model was introduced by Thornycroft in 1957 for loads of 6 to 7 tons and this very long-wheelbase version, with its Boalloy-style plastics cab, must surely have impressed the neighbours when it arrived in the little town of Rhymney in the autumn of 1960. Rhymney Breweries have an interesting logo consisting of a huntsman riding a horse whose body is a beer cask, and a little model of this can be seen atop the cab. This photo was taken in the yard of Rhymney Breweries during the winter, when it had done a few months' work.

'From the cold of a Scandinavian winter to the blazing heat of an African sun, Austin trucks are ubiquitous, taking in their ample stride all the variations in climate, terrain and duty which must be undergone in serving the transport needs of all nations.' So runs the introduction to Austin's sales brochure for the Fifties – a little wordier than their traditional 'Austin – you can depend on it' slogan! Austin supplied, as a standard model, a stake and chain-sided brewer's dray but this Whitbread model, which entered service on May 3, 1957, had a body built to Whitbread's specification by Express Motor Bodies Ltd. Overall dimensions of this version included a 12ft 3in-long body within a 19ft 6in overall length, 7ft 4in width and 7ft 3in height. The platform, which carried a 3-ton payload, was only 3ft 7in high and unladen weight was 2 ton 8cwt 101lb (2,490kg). This slightly later model was fitted with BMC's own four-cylinder diesel engine, but earlier versions had the option of Austin's 4-litre OHV truck engine which developed 174lb/ft of torque at only 1,000rpm or the Perkins P6 (at extra cost!) which developed 204lb/ft of torque at the same revs. Heavier models in this range, from 5 tons upwards, were offered with an Eaton two-speed axle, a fairly advanced feature for trucks in this weight category at the time.

By 1958, a full 10 years after the model FT3L, Albion 6 to 7-tonners looked like this one which entered service in July of that year. At first glance there has been hardly any development at all, but closer inspection shows that this FT37 KCL is now altogether more refined. The cab has a more streamlined and better finished appearance, with integral headlamps, but still has only one windscreen wiper. The body is functional with folding steps on the leading side of the headboard to allow access to the load for sheeting. With an unladen weight of 3 ton 6cwt 3qr 21lb (3,408kg) and a payload of 6 tons 10cwt (6,618kg) the previously mentioned gross:tare ratio has dropped to 2.94:1, an improvement of over 20% on the first attempt, but falling short of the FT3L's figure by over 10%.

It is difficult to see where the additional weight has been incurred on the 1948 FT37 KCL model: it has the same engine as previously – the Albion diesel – and the body appears to be no heavier even though it has an extra 8sq ft of deck, so perhaps the difference is accounted for by unseen provisions for the extra half-ton payload in such areas as, for example, the suspension.

Dennis Bros had introduced the Pax III by the late Fifties which was widely used on delivery work, having a payload of 7½ tons. This vehicle, VGF 986, entered service on June 17, 1958 and is of interest since it so clearly shows the lengths to which designers had to go to improve productivity. In this case the deck-height has been lowered to the extent that wheelboxes are required, and whilst this makes the task of lifting cases off the vehicle simpler, it makes loading rather more complicated since there is no flat surface, and a degree of juggling is required to make the load sit still and square. This particular vehicle is very unlikely to have been used for cask beers as it was customary to have sides of some description for load retention in view of the much greater unit weights.

Before articulated vehicles gained in popularity, as a result of a legislative change allowing 32 tons gross weight, all heavy goods work was carried out by 'eight leggers'. Seen here loading cased beer – one case at a time because this was before pallets were introduced on a wide scale – is the very elegant Gardner diesel-engined Scammell R8 which was operated on contract for Whitbread & Co. Scammell, whose eight-wheeler was lighter than any of the competition to allow greater payloads, used different-sized tyres, front and rear, on many of their models – and this practice persisted for many years. It may have been instrumental in their gaining a reputation for being a high-speed trunk vehicle, but this was more likely to have arisen from their low unladen weight. Note the retractable dock-conveyor running onto the vehicle to cut down the amount of perambulation required to assemble a load.

A rather better view of the Scammell R8, just having completed loading at the bottling plant. Of all the eight-wheelers available at the time, the Scammell had the furthest set-forward front axle, a feature which in some observers' views, detracts from its general appearance. However, to the enthusiast, the real joy of this vehicle was to hear it: powered by the so-called 'legendary Gardner' this vehicle positively purred and, when on tickover, it was possible to hear the metal joint in the fan belt on each engine revolution. This shot was taken in about 1950 by which time the Leyland Hippo on the right – also on contract, but this time from W Arnold and Sons, who did quite a lot of brewery work – would have seen a good few years' service. The vehicle in the centre is the 6-ton Dennis Lancet and is clearly the most recent of the three shown. The retractable loading conveyors can be seen on Number 2 and Number 3 docks as can some overhead conveyoring leading into the plant.

After the civilian O-types for 3 to 5-ton working, and S-type for 7-ton working, Bedford introduced the A-type, which had forward control and was available for 25cwt to 5-ton payloads with a petrol or diesel option. The A-type was produced from 1953 to 1957 and was followed by what was commonly called the J-type, officially the Bedford TJ, which was very similar in appearance and was produced from 1959 to 1975.

The vehicle illustrated, with its Gloucestershire registration, dates from the middle of 1960. Available for 25cwt to 7-ton working, the TJ also had the option of a petrol or a diesel engine. West Country Breweries opted for the long-wheelbase diesel version for operation at 7 tons and, with such a long vehicle, it probably earned its nickname 'the swing-nosed J-type'.

CHAPTER FIVE

Artics, Drawbars, Tanks and Tankers

The continual quest for improved performance, efficiency and productivity suggested quite early on that a good way to gain payload was to pull a trailer, and there were several ideas about how best to do that!

Horse-drawn equipment was strictly of the trailer-pulling type and this method was copied by traction engines where a steam-powered vehicle simply replaced the horse – or horses, for the engines of course were much more powerful. However, as already seen, traction engines gave way first to steam and later to motor-lorries which *carried* rather than pulled the load.

To gain real productivity improvements it was thought sensible both to carry a load *and* to pull one, and two major contenders appeared with a further subsidiary one to fulfil this role. They were, in chronological sequence, the articulated vehicle which, surprisingly perhaps, dates back to the 19th century, and the drawbar trailer, also known variously as 'waggon and drag' or 'dolly and dangler'.

The subsidiary idea was a hybrid of both types, developed by Pagefield, in which part of the load was imposed upon the drawing unit – a necessary condition for an artic – for part of the time, but which transferred the weight under certain braking, acceleration and loading conditions to make the combination more like a drawbar unit. This did not really catch on and no records have been found of its sustained use in breweries – probably no bad thing as it was not the easiest vehicle to drive, if only because the gearbox had a side-to-side change-speed action. This would have entailed a degree of retraining which would have been relatively expensive for so little, if any, advantage. To celebrate their centenary year the Marks and Spencer group restored a Pagefield to full working condition and the opportunity should be taken to see this interesting vehicle.

But to return to artics: the idea of an articulated vehicle dates back to as early as 1896 when Thornycroft came up with a permanently coupled articulated trailer attached to a modified lorry as a drawing unit. The idea, however, was slow to gain acceptance in the UK and even slower in Europe where, due to the vagaries of transport legislation, drawbars were preferred. Little solid progress was made until, in 1933, Scammell announced at the Olympia Motor Show their 'mechanical horse' which became so well-loved by the railway companies. The mechanical horse was also developed simultaneously by Karrier, who later sold out their patents to Scammell. These vehicles consisted of a three-wheeled articulated tractor unit with a very small (10 RAC horsepower or about 1,000–1,300cc) side-valve petrol engine. They could turn in their own length and were widely used for luggage collection and delivery under the old railway CL, DL and PLA system. (The railways used to operate a system by which passengers could send their luggage independently under one of three schemes: CL covered collection and conveyance; DL covered conveyance and delivery and PLA covered collection, conveyance and delivery).

As an interesting aside, these 'Scarabs' enjoyed a good export trade and in the late Fifties they could be seen in vast numbers, bringing tea to the docks in Colombo harbour. This particular operation appeared haphazard, but must have been a masterpiece of organization as the little vehicles scurried about like ants in a disturbed nest and, using their trailer quick-release gear, drivers deftly dropped trailers loaded with tea-chests and picked up empty ones, all without leaving the cab, at the same time as avoiding the large loading nets swinging in great arcs from the ships' derricks.

Brewers made use of mechanical horses at about 3 to 5 or 6-tons payload, as did many other trades, but compared with today artics were a tiny proportion of the nation's fleet and mostly confined to relatively light work. The real benefit of articulation lies, as with the Colombo docks

A typical Scammell product of the period, this chain-driven artic supplied to Allsopp's Brewery, Burton on Trent, in 1926 actually shows many refinements over earlier Spitalfields-produced models. It not only has a windscreen – few were fitted on this model or its predecessors before 1920 – but also an enclosed cab, albeit a rather crude affair but a distinct improvement over the canvas cab which was all that was on offer right up to 1922. It is also equipped with electric lighting although the lamps appear to be fitted on the lugs previously provided for acetylene lamps. Contemporary catalogues list this as being a 10-tonner capable, even in artic configuration, *of pulling a trailer with an additional 5-tons payload*, a configuration known as a 'double bottom' or 'B'-train which, today, is not allowed in the UK without a special licence granted for each journey. Operating costs for the rig as shown were advertised as being 1s 2d (6p) per mile and 1d (less than 0.4p) per ton-mile.

This tail-end view of a 1934 Leyland Cub artic poses some questions. The trailer, manufactured by Crane – later to become Crane Fruehauf – is undoubtedly of a type used by brewers, having an attachment for a barrel-skid at the rear, but has a modified headboard which is curved to allow extra-close coupling, a feature which was uncommon in brewery operation. Moreover, the tractor unit is almost totally obscured by what appears to be a metal partition, which suggests compliance with petroleum regulations. Could this be a brewer's vehicle commandeered for the war effort? However, the condition of the trailer and what can be seen of the unit suggests that it is new and the date is reputedly 1934, so this seems unlikely.

example, in the ability to leave an empty trailer for loading whilst the tractor unit pulls a laden trailer doing useful work. Artic trailers are, strictly, *semi*-trailers, as part of the load (at least 20% by law) is imposed upon the drawing vehicle and it is this condition which defines for legislative purposes an articulated vehicle.

Articulation really came into its own in this country when the law was changed to allow operation at 32 tons gross combination weight (GCW), thus giving an advantage over the eight-wheeler which, even in the early Nineties,

was still restricted for on-road operation in the UK to 30 tons GVW (gross vehicle weight).

In many ways articulation was used more intelligently in the early days than it is today when, much of the time, they are simply used to enable operation at the highest possible gross weight.

Drawbar combinations, in which a more-or-less standard lorry pulls a separate trailer, were popular in Great Britain from the early days of motorized transport up to about the time of the Second World War. By that time large-capacity

An early example of the 'mechanical horse' type of artic, this 'Cob' produced by Karrier Motors was operated at about 3-tons payload by Davenport's Brewery at Bath Row, Birmingham, in the Thirties. The legend on the side of the cab tells us that its speed was restricted to 16mph or, with the trailer, 8mph, so this would only have been effective on runs which were fairly local to the brewery. Although unfortunately the negative is damaged, it is still possible to see some of the detail of the ratcheted brake mechanism for when the trailer was left standing and of the turntable with its handwheel release gear – so different from Scammell's quick-release patent. The chain between the cab and the trailer is part of the background and nothing to do with the vehicle itself!

Dating from just after the war, being registered in Manchester sometime between September 1945 and March 1947, this imported Chevrolet was operated by Chesters at about 5 to 6-tons payload. Very similar in detail to the Bedford O-types and, unusually, in right-hand drive specification, this handsome unit is pulling a purpose-built brewery trailer. Note the strengthened corner-posts and the 'boxing-ring' body; also, tucked away in a bracket beneath the tailboard, the ends of the barrel-skid can just be seen. Ropes and spare wheel are stowed down by the fifth-wheel coupling and a 'trug' or 'bogie' is thrown atop the load – along with an opened case of wines or spirits which looks precariously balanced.

Brand names in the Fifties abounded with corrupted spellings even in the transport industry – this was the era of, amongst others, the Kleer-Vu cab and, in keeping with the times, Dennis chose the unattractive name 'Horla' for their artic tractor. Dennis had been major suppliers of vehicles to the brewery trade for many years and this normal-control Horla of 1954 vintage is an example of one of their early offerings in artic form. Although the vehicle in the photo was used for soft drinks delivery, it is identical in most respects with those used by brewers. It is matched to a Scammell trailer and the quick-coupling gear can clearly be seen. From this position the procedure was to reverse the unit on to the trailer so that the small wheels, just below the load platform, engaged on the lead-in ramps. Assuming that the trailer brake was on, the mechanism simply folded up and dropped into a catch which was secured from inside the cab. Trailer-braking was provided by vacuum hydraulics operated by a lever acting on a tongue-lever mounted between the jockey wheels. A rod connected to the tongue-lever then operated the trailer master-cylinder. The trailer's lighting – sidelights, stoplights and indicators – was provided, fully automatically without the use of 'susies', by contact plates between the tractor and the coupling.

rigid vehicles offered substantial payloads and, not many years later, artics began to emerge as the big load carriers. In Europe, drawbars retained their popularity all along and the idea developed to a higher degree of sophistication than in the UK. In recent years the pendulum has swung and drawbars are experiencing a revival.

Using an expression like 'a more-or-less standard lorry' is possibly misleading. In appearance, without the trailer connected, it is not immediately apparent that a vehicle is equipped for drawbar operation and, indeed, it looks like a standard lorry. But usually a larger engine is required to cope with the increased weight, not only of the payload, of course, but of the trailer and, to a limited extent, of the larger engine! Brakes require modification, again to cope with increased loads; tyres, transmission and suspension may need uprating and, obviously, a coupling connection –

a hook in its simplest guise – must be fitted.

Some interesting legislative quirks surround drawbar units. For example, the maximum permissible weight for drawbar trailer combinations was the same in 1992 as it was during the war, when it was raised to permit ammunition 'trains' on the roads to be moved more efficiently. In the Forties it was raised to 32 tons, a limit which has remained unchanged into the early Nineties – a perfect example of how legislation can affect productivity – and international competition! Also, for some reason, drawbar combinations could be driven by holders of the old Class III Heavy Goods Vehicle Driver's Licence which covered vehicles over 7½ tonnes GVW on two axles only. Whilst being far more difficult to manoeuvre, particularly in reverse, than an artic, it required no additional training to hold a licence – and no additional test!

The trailers themselves are of several different types, traditionally having four wheels – one at each corner – and steerable either by a rotating turntable or by the more sophisticated – and more predictable – Ackermann steering. More recently trailers have appeared with four wheels close-coupled like a caravan, but these appeared after the time currently being discussed.

An old trunk-driver once told me a story about a wartime journey he had made through the New Forest at night with masked headlamps, flat-out with a full load *and* a fully laden trailer. His 'waggon' was an eight-wheeler, an Armstrong-Saurer, and his 'drag', a flat platform loaded to the limit and tarpaulin-sheeted. He described the thrill of 'really clipping along' through the dark forest and, when asked what 'clipping along' meant in those days, he declared a speed of nearly 24mph!

Drawbar trailers were not widely used by breweries although they occasionally played a part in transfer or long-haul work. The few illustrations available of drawbars in brewery use show about the only possibilities which exist – open trailers, closed boxvans and tankers.

The ultimate step for productivity, as measured by how much *beer* it was possible to carry on any particular vehicle, had to be to carry beer alone – without any packaging at all.

Bottled beer represents the least productive way to transport beer: half a pint of beer is enclosed in a glass bottle which weighs nearly as much as the beer it contains; the bottle is then put into – until comparatively recently – a wooden case which, in the worst instance, might have been put on to a wooden pallet for loading. The load then had to be secured with ropes and, possibly, tarpaulin sheets. Not only that, but bottles are round with narrow tops so there are large air spaces between and around them, hence the load was made up, to a large extent, of packaging and air with only a minority of it actually being the product requiring transport!

Most productive of all – measured in terms of quantity of actual beer per vehicle – was the eight-wheeler, in which 80 barrels (2,880gall or over 23,000pt) of beer were transported – with only one driver. After legislation changed to allow 32-tons GCW operation, articulated tankers of 120 barrels (4,320gall) capacity became commonplace and attention then turned to how to make them yet more productive still by speeding up the loading and discharge operations.

Several clever ideas were tried to overcome the fact that beer tends to 'fob' – the industry term for frothing – when it is moved about, particularly whilst filling or discharging tanks, casks or even bottles. Some of the tanks illustrated have metal helmets which were part of the apparatus required for a gas cover over the beer. The fermentation process, in which yeast converts sugars into alcohol, gives off quantities of carbon dioxide (CO_2), which in some breweries is exhausted into the atmosphere. In others it is retained and used to pressurize the tankers before loading, which not only keeps the beer in first-class condition but also helps keep the fob down.

Other ideas included having a very steep slant on the tank, thus reducing the surface area available to fob. Yet others were bottom-filled so that the liquid itself restrained the fobbing. All were successful in their own way but the most successful of all was a combination of all three in which a slanted tank was pre-pressurized and filled from underneath.

Care had to be taken that loading was carefully supervised in another sense, too. Occasionally, beer would be moved in a part-processed condition – a wort which was not fully fermented for example or, in the case of the heavier beers and stouts, fully fermented but in an unfined condition. Pure water weighs 10lb per gallon; the lightest of lagers weighs a fraction more, but a heavy stout – like Guinness, for example, especially in unfined condition, weighs very considerably more.

A 120-barrel tanker filled with pure water would hold just over 19¼ tons (19 ton 5cwt 2qr 24lb). The maximum payload available within the old 32-ton limit was just over 20 tons – the tractor unit, the trailer and the tank itself accounting for the other 12 tons – so there was often only about a three or four percent margin before becoming overloaded!

A part-loaded tanker has an increased tendency to fobbing and experiments were carried out with table-tennis balls filling the ullage space to reduce this problem. The experiments were successful in two ways: they reduced fobbing and they demonstrated that the ping-pong balls were not such a brilliant idea because they took a great deal of cleaning between loads!

However, they did also reduce another slightly unpleasant characteristic of tankers. When a tanker stops, the load surges forward to the front end of the tank and an unwary driver can be caught out by his vehicle which, having stopped – at traffic lights for example – suddenly leaps forward. Even when fully prepared, it is quite noticeable. In modern vessels the problem has been overcome by the fitting of baffles which reduce the large forward movement to a series of smaller ones.

In spite of the huge gains in productivity made by tankers, they did, of course, also have disadvantages. Tankers are, unquestionably, special-purpose vehicles; they carry bulk liquids – or, in some industries, powders – but nothing else. They cannot, therefore, be used for backloading anything other than bulk liquids – or powders. Even if a return load is available the product must be compatible with what is usually carried and, even if it is totally compatible, as for example a return load of another type of beer might appear to be, the tank has to be cleaned before it can be refilled. It is, therefore, a feature of tanker operation in breweries that the return journey is usually empty: empty, that is, except for 'caustic', the cleaning agent which is used for all brewery tank containers to ensure that no alien yeasts or other impurities can affect the next load.

Tanks were used in all sorts of configurations, rigid, articulated, drawbar and even demountable, and in spite of their disadvantages, they remain to this day an effective and efficient way of moving beer – or any liquid product for that matter – in bulk.

Seddon enjoyed considerable popularity with brewers for the heavier categories of work. Seddons were beautifully built and this 1954 Perkins P6-engined version is very evocative of the era. This vehicle has a cab built by Marshalls of Cambridge which is rather unusual as Seddons built their own cabs for the UK market. The vehicle shown was modified in March 1958 by exchanging the old coupling gear – presumably Scammell automatic – for the heavier duty and more up-to-date fifth-wheel type coupling. Modifications of such magnitude would seldom be contemplated today on a vehicle nearly four years old. The records show that the tractor unit was 14ft 3in long overall, 8ft 2in wide including the mirrors and 8ft 3in high. From the centre of the kingpin to the rear of the cab measured 6ft exactly (hence the need for a curved front-end to the trailer) and from the end of the chassis to the rear of the cab was 9ft 2in. The trailer, which was built by Carrimores Ltd, first saw service in April 1955 but it, too, was modified in March 1958 by the fitting of new coupling gear. It was also equipped with a Model 11 (2-ton) horizontal winch with a preset safety brake and 60ft of wire rope supplied by Thompson Bros (Engineers) Ltd and fitted by Carrimores. This indicates that the rig may have been used for recovery of stranded vehicles and for the movement, between depots, of fork-lift trucks; certainly the winch was not a 'standard extra'! Its overall length and width were 26ft 8in and 7ft 9in respectively. Bulkhead to end of first platform was 12ft 6in; step to second platform, 1ft 3in; rear platform length was 14ft 2in and its height was 3ft 3in. The trailer weighed 3 ton 9cwt and the tractor 3 ton 1cwt – a truly remarkable combination.

Another example of the Dennis Horla, operated by Whitbread on transfer work to and from Romford Road, Manor Park in London. These photos show the traditional three poses which were commonly taken for the record and which form a large part of the author's collection.

This particular vehicle had a payload capacity of 7 tons on a normal-sided trailer measuring 20ft long by 7ft 6in wide and it entered service on May 31, 1954.

Yet another Horla, included to show a slightly ill-proportioned design for only 5-tons payload. This vehicle entered service at Lewisham depot on June 19, 1956 (although the record is very strict in recording that the trailer didn't manage it until the following day!) and was used for delivery rather than transfer work. Diesel-engined for economy and with a Hands trailer of only 16ft long, this would have been a handy dray for those awkward deliveries in inaccessible places, and was thus the forerunner of the urban artic, a concept perfected by Bass many years later. This rather untidy-looking vehicle has what appears to be bits of scrap metal hanging down all over the place. These in fact are metal stops to prevent the dropsides hitting the coachwork or damaging the tyre sidewalls.

Still with Dennis, but looking much more modern even though it dates from the same time as the Horla, this Dennis Centaur 10-tonner went into service in Leicester on September 7, 1956. Used for transfer work, this straightforward and businesslike rig exhibits a number of interesting features. The platform is canted so that palletized loads of crates lean towards the centre-line, thus enhancing stability. There is a mini-tailboard which can be lowered to clear the barrel-skid attachment – which looks as if it has worked for its living! Webbing straps are provided, with hooks to go right under the rave so that they do not snag clothes or equipment, and tarpaulin sheets are neatly stowed away on a special platform at the top of the headboard.

Another Horla used for delivery work, this diesel-powered 6-tonner entered service on December 12, 1957. The idea behind the dropframe 19in deck-height trailer was to ease the draymen's task of unloading, compared with the conventional-height platform, although the photo showing the laden condition begs the question of how it achieved this aim as the top cases were a long way from the ground.

Note that the load is palletized to simplify loading, which would have been carried out by a fork-lift truck in the yard – necessary because the low deck-height rendered the trailer incompatible with the loading dock at the depot – every silver lining has its cloud!

The designers must have learned much from this experimental version; the well, which measured 15ft by 7ft 5in, was not quite right even for the over-size brewery pallets; it was not possible to load a pallet on the high front platform; the wheelbox top was too small to take a pallet and the pallet which went between the wheelboxes was not a good fit either. However, the purpose of experimental vehicles was to find out things such as this.

The Dennis Maxim was introduced in the early Sixties and by 1966 was offered for 30-ton gross applications for which it would no doubt have been rather short of power, in its standard form, having only some 165bhp. BLH 521B is seen in 1964 on test around the Guildford area, loaded with concrete blocks. The model remained largely unchanged for several years and the influence of the fire appliance design is quite clear. Just discernible on the fuel tank is the vehicle's unladen weight of 4 ton 9cwt 1qr (4,544kg) which probably accounts for its popularity as a low-weight tractive unit. Photos courtesy of Dennis Brothers Ltd, Guildford.

At first glance, the outward appearance of the bodies on this mid-Thirties Leyland operated by Watneys suggests that they are demountable which would make them representative of some of the latest thinking in this field. However, closer inspection denies this as there are no shackles or other provision for lifting and no apparent fitments for securing the body. The outfit is fairly typical with the drawing unit carrying a heavier load than the trailer – typically in the ratio 7:5 or 5:3. The date of this photo is not known but it seems clear that the tyres are not OE (original equipment), having been enhanced to take the extra load. The trailer appears to be of much later vintage, probably dating from around 1946–7.

Right: Latil was a French company (Automobiles Industriels Latil, of Seresne) which, just before the First World War, introduced an all-wheel drive, all-wheel steer tractor for military use, which remained in production until about 1920. In the Thirties, several civilian models were introduced amongst which was the Traulier, which was produced in a Belgian plant in Brussels as well as under licence in the UK by Shelvoke and Drewry, noted more for their municipal vehicles and refuse collectors. Aimed primarily at round-timber hauliers, it found favour with such diverse operators as the railways and Union Cartage for meat haulage from the docks as well as many others. Typically, with any new idea, the brewers became actively interested and evaluated them for brewery use. A favourite trick of the experienced hands was to park one against a wall with all the wheels steered inwards and then to ask a novice 'just to bring the Traulier round, please'.

Latil ceased production altogether in 1956 having joined forces with Renault and Somua to form Saviem in 1955.

90

As might be expected for this era, Whitbread used Dennis as the prime mover for their relatively few drawbar units. This 1948 photo shows a Dennis 5 to 7-tonner hauling a – probably Task-built – trailer of 3 to 5-tons capacity. Air-braking is used, as witness the hoses connecting the two units. The trailer is number T3, which suggests that there were at least three drawbars in the fleet and the fact that the prime mover needed at least some modifications is evidenced by the coupling gear adjacent to the (permanently fixed) starting handle. Drawbar trailers are notoriously difficult to control whilst reversing – quite unlike an artic, they 'bend' both at the coupling and at the turntable – so it was common practice to uncouple the trailer and recouple it to the hook at the front so that the trailer could be 'nosed in'.

This shows an interesting use of 'waggon-and-drag' or drawbar-trailer use. Photographed late on a winter's afternoon outside the Green Dragon public house in the mid-Fifties, the Thornycroft 'waggon' is loaded with cased beer – including Glucose Stout which would not have been available in casks – whilst the 'drag' carries barrels of George's ales from the old Bristol brewery. George's brewery was later acquired by the Courage group to be merged with their own interests in the area. Experiments by brewers with drawbar trailers have been an occasional feature of the brewery transport scene right through to the Nineties and even now there is nothing to show that the ideal (brewery) configuration has yet been developed. The photograph shows a four-man crew engaged in unloading the delivery, which suggests that either the shot has been posed specially to publicize a newly delivered vehicle or that some extraordinary economics are at work to justify such labour intensiveness!

ERF OIL ENGINED TRACTORS

LEADING DIMENSIONS :				Model L.K.4.4.	Model 4.4.	Model 5.4.	Model 6.4.
WHEELBASE. Std.				8′ – 8″	8′ – 2″	8′ – 5″	8′ – 7″
TYRES. Std.	FRONT			8.25″ × 20″	10.00″ × 20″	10.00″ × 20″	10.00″ × 20″
,, ,,	REAR			34″ × 7″	36″ × 8″	36″ × 8″	36″ × 8″
ENGINE.				4 LK	4 LW	5 LW	6 LW
Bore and Stroke				3¾″ × 5¼″	4¼″ × 6″	4¼″ × 6″	4¼″ × 6″
Piston Displacement				232 cu. ins.	340 cu. ins.	425 cu. ins.	510 cu. ins.
B.H.P. (@ r.p.m. (max.)				53 @ 2,000	75 @ 1,700	94 @ 1,700	112 @ 1,700
Torque lbs. ft. @ r.p.m.				147 @ 1,200	237 @ 1,000	300 @ 1,000	358 @ 1,000
R.A.C. rating				22½	29	36½	43½
CLUTCH Diameter				12″	14″	16″	16″
GEARBOX				542	045	557	557
	5th			1.	.75	1.	1.
	4th			1.6	1.	1.565	1.565
TRANSMISSION Ratios.	3rd			2.79	1.795	2.74	2.74
	2nd			4.73	3.24	4.68	4.68
	1st			8.14	6.09	7.92	7.92
	Rev.			7.76	5.98	7.92	7.92
REAR AXLE Ratio Std.				6.5	8.25	7.25	7.25
BRAKES area.							
Foot—four wheels				384 sq. in.	512 sq. in.	512 sq. in.	512 sq. in.
Hand—two ,,				224 sq. in.	320 sq. in.	320 sq. in.	320 sq. in.
Fuel Tank capacity				20 gallons	33 gallons	33 gallons	33 gallons
Fuel consumption				20-24 m.p.g.	18-20 m.p.g.	14-16 m.p.g.	10-12 m.p.g.
Length overall				13′ – 4″	13′ – 4″	13′ – 9″	14′ – 0″
Width ,,				7′ – 0″	7′ – 5¾″	7′ – 5¾″	7′ – 5¾″
Height ,, (with Cab)				7′ – 5½″	8′ – 3½″	8′ – 3½″	8′ – 3½″
Track front at ground				5′ – 7⅞″	6′ – 4½″	6′ – 4½″	6′ – 4½″
,, rear				5′ – 5½″	5′ – 8½″	5′ – 8″	5′ – 8″
Frame height loaded				3′ – 3″	3′ – 5″	3′ – 5″	3′ – 5″
Turning Circle				38′ – 0″	34′ – 6″	36′ – 0″	37′ – 0″
Unladen Weight (Chassis only)				2 tons 6 cwts.	3 tons 10 cwts.	3 tons 12 cwts.	3 tons 14 cwts.
	5th			34.25 m.p.h.	30.8 m.p.h.	26.2 m.p.h.	26.2 m.p.h.
Road Speeds	4th			21.40 ,,	23. ,,	16.74 ,,	16.74 ,,
@ max. r.p.m.	3rd			12.25 ,,	12.85 ,,	9.56 ,,	9.56 ,,
and Std. Axle	2nd			7.23 ,,	7.11 ,,	5.6 ,,	5.6 ,,
Ratio	1st			4.20 ,,	3.79 ,,	3.3 ,,	3.3 ,,
	Rev.			4.41 ,,	3.86 ,,	3.3 ,,	3.3 ,,

Although not widely used by the brewing industry, at least until recent times, ERF warrants inclusion in the story of advancing productivity if only for the way in which the company came about. The initials ERF stand for Edwin Richard Foden, who was a close relative of the founders of the old-established Foden company. In the very early Thirties it became obvious to some manufacturers that the new-fangled 'oil' engines (diesels) were the thing of the future, having many advantages over steam. The board of directors of the Foden company thought, however, that there was still a good living to be made by sticking to the tried and proven steam technology. In the event, one of the younger generation of Fodens contacted his semi-retired uncle, who was sheep farming in Australia, and persuaded him to return to England to start manufacturing 'oilers'. This he did, just down the road from the Foden works in Sandbach, the first vehicles being badged as E R Fodens, to which a quick visit to the law-courts soon put a stop! This reproduction of ERF's 1950 sales literature makes an interesting comparison with the technical specifications of some of today's artic tractors – especially with only between 53 and 112bhp on offer, compared with figures around and above the 300bhp mark, and even 400bhp and above for intercontinental work, now.

Seen parked in Madeira Drive, Brighton, on the Historic Commercial Vehicle Society's London to Brighton run, this Scammell Scarab makes an interesting comparison with the Mechanical Horse on page 81. This one, restored in the livery of Bulmers Cider, was registered in London and dates from October 1959. Best known for their work in connection with the railway companies, Scarabs were used by several brewers for deliveries which were not too distant from the brewery. Scarab models were available for either 3 or 6-ton working and these differed mechanically from the previous model, the Scammell MH – which the Scarab replaced in 1948 – by having the engine and gearbox situated very low behind the cab. In 1964 the Scarab was in turn replaced by the Townsman which had, some would say, an over-styled glassfibre cab and Leyland diesel engine, Scammell being, by then, part of the Leyland group.

By the early Fifties Bedford were established as regular suppliers of vehicles to the brewery trade. In 1951 they introduced the S-type – whose general appearance is probably best known as the so-called Green Goddess fire appliances which were built on the four-wheel-drive chassis supplied to the armed forces and known as the R-type or, more commonly, the Bedford RL. Even though the civilian S-types were available with a petrol or diesel option and had several very desirable features about them, few were used on delivery work by brewers. Their nickname, the 'Big Bedford', was earned by being the heaviest vehicle which Vauxhall had ever produced in the UK, and it is this feature which probably best suited them to some of the ancillary roles which they played in brewing. Bedford had a long-standing association with Scammell for producing artics, many Bedford-Scammells having been used by all three of the armed forces during the war. A 'Big' Bedford-Scammell tractor unit was offered (from 1951 to 1960, when the model was superseded), for 10-ton payload, giving a maximum gross combination weight of 14 tons. The main photograph shows one of the uses to which it was put, carrying hops for Fremlins of Maidstone, each hopsack weighing just over 2cwt (130kg). To the right are details of the Scammell automatic coupling.

94

Some relatively early rigid tankers on Saurer chassis. Little is known about this photograph: the vehicles appear to be UK-operated, having right-hand drive and British registration marks, but Saurer was a 'continental' truck producer (originally Swiss, but later setting up companies in both Austria and France). The photo was taken at a brewery site and, whilst Whitbread had premises in Brussels, they were only distribution depot facilities. Even at the time of this photo, which shows vehicles with bulb-horns and acetylene lighting, Whitbread's UK fleet numbering system included a prefix letter from which the vehicle manufacturer could be identified, yet the vehicle nearest the camera is No 37, not S37 as might be expected (except that the letter 'S' was allocated to Seddon!) or Sa37, which was Whitbread's way round duplicated initial letters.

The tanks appear to be of stainless steel and of around 20 barrels capacity, giving a payload of just over 3 tons which, with the weight of the tank, would be about right for this vehicle.

Fitted with a tank of almost identical construction to those on the Saurers, this 1935 Albion 5-tonner also exhibits the mysterious fleet numbering anomaly. To bring it a little more up to date, it has had some apparatus added for gas pressure relief and the attendant, whose dress has changed markedly from the days of the old-style draymen, also looks more modern. He appears to be operating a handwheel in preparation for discharging the load, a somewhat simpler, less tiring and hence more productive way to unload than hefting large casks.

A typical 40-barrel (1,440gall) tanker on a rigid Dennis chassis, this vehicle was fitted with the Dennis six-cylinder diesel known as the 'O6' and entered service between Whitbread's London brewery and satellite bottling plants on June 22, 1954. The cab was manufactured and fitted by Sparshatts of Portsmouth and the vessel by Burnett & Rolfe Ltd. Its overall dimensions were 24ft 4in long, 9ft 4in high and 7ft 7in wide: unladen, this vehicle tipped the scales at 5 ton 19cwt, thus grossing around 12½ tons, depending upon the product carried.

Fitted with an identical Burnett & Rolfe 40-barrel vessel, Whitbread also used Seddon chassis for the same task as the Dennis. Interestingly, the sideboards on the Seddon point out that it was used for the transport of Mackeson Stout, a product with a much higher specific gravity and therefore much heavier than bitter and lager beers. This is reflected in the unladen weight of only 5 ton 11cwt, a full 8cwt lighter than the Dennis.

There are other details which make this a decidedly upmarket option compared with the workaday Dennis: the Seddon De Luxe cab was fitted and, in the engine department, the magnificent Gardner 5LW. Dimensionally, the Seddon was a fraction smaller than the Dennis, being an inch narrower at 7ft 6in and 14in shorter at 23ft 2in.

The rear view is of interest, showing the handwheel for opening the access door for tank-cleaning and, on the rear end of the chassis, the coupling for a drawbar trailer which is mounted on a laminated spring. The two flattened metal pieces either side of the hook are to enable an operator to open the coupling with his foot whilst manhandling the heavy trailer coupling. The letters RT in the fleet number denote Rigid Tanker; options were TT for Trailer Tank, AT for Articulated Tank and CT for Compartmented Tank.

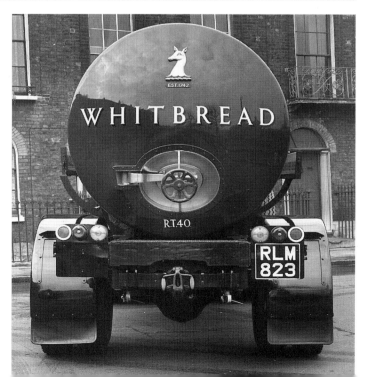

Both Atkinson and AEC eight-wheeled chassis were used for mounting maximum-capacity, 80-barrel (2,880gall nominal) tanks and a selection is shown on these two pages.

Left: Oldest of the batch is the Mark III AEC which dates from March 1951 and which was fitted with the 9.6-litre AEC 'oil engine'. The cab was by Marshalls of Cambridge and, typically for Whitbread, the tank was by Burnett & Rolfe. With an unladen weight, according to the records, of 8 ton 17cwt (9,010kg) but with 8 ton 6cwt 1qr 8lb (8,467kg) painted on the side, this model measured 30ft long, 7ft 6in wide and was 10ft 2in high overall. The total unladen weight on the front pair of axles was 4 ton 10cwt 3qr 21lb (4,630kg) which without power assistance to the steering must have been quite hard work. The rear bogie, unladen, carried 3 ton 16cwt 2qr (3,895kg) and the vehicle was restricted to 30mph.

Rather more up to date is the AEC Mark V, seen lower left. Special features are the glassfibre cab built by Holmes of Preston in February 1959 and the glassfibre helmet cover which was home-made by the operator in the following month. Note how, even in 1959, no attempt has been made to lower the centre of gravity for stability purposes. There are several ways of doing this, including use of tanks of oval cross-section, something which has never caught on in brewery work. Other methods include mounting the tank lower between the chassis longitudinals, but this often means using single rear wheels which, in turn, usually means adding another axle to take the weight. As with all improvements, there is a price to pay.

The observant reader will have noticed that this vehicle's registration mark, LYF 995, follows immediately the Mark III's number LYF 994. For some licensing authorities it was the practice to issue large fleet operators with batches of numbers for them to allocate themselves. Whitbread was such an operator, being large enough even to carry all its own insurance and, it appears, keep batches of numbers for allocation to vehicles with specific duties.

Right: This Gardner 6LW-powered five-speed glassfibre-cabbed Atkinson carries an 80-barrel tank manufactured by Thompson (Bilston) Ltd. Unusually for its year, this vehicle was fitted with power-assisted steering so it must have been a joy to drive, especially when compared with the noisy, draughty, unheated Mark III AECs. This vehicle weighed in, unladen, at 9 ton 4cwt, so grossed about 22 tons; it entered service on July 9, 1958.

Similar in many respects, this February 1960 model Atkinson, centre right, differs by having the AEC 9.6-litre diesel engine fitted. It also has a Ramsden's tank and is 4in longer at 30ft 4in; an inch narrower at 7ft 7in and an inch lower at 10ft 2in. It is also much heavier at 9 ton 11cwt 2qr 15lb (9,737kg compared with 9,367kg).

Records for the vehicle lower right have been lost, but it is of considerable interest because Seddon traditionally produced four-wheelers at their factory at Oldham, Lancs. Further down the road at Preston, Atkinson produced vehicles at the heavier end of the weight range and, to make both the smaller companies into a larger force which could be reckoned with worldwide, the two companies merged in the mid-Seventies to form Seddon Atkinson. The rest, as they say, is history.

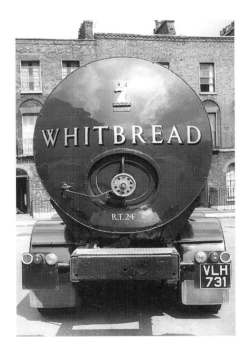

We have already seen that Dennis were major suppliers of vehicles to the brewery trade and, in fact, there is probably a Dennis example of every configuration which was ever tried! This example, sometimes affectionately known as 'the pig', is the normal-control version of the artic tanker although the unit started work with a conventional trailer, the tank trailer dating from September 1949. Unusually, the cab shows the fleet letter 'H', which may have been an error on the part of the fleet administrator, since Dennis should have had 'D' as their prefix; perhaps this 'H' stood for Horla, which is the model name. Originally into service on May 30, 1949 with a Dennis six-cylinder petrol engine, this little artic was converted to diesel by having a Perkins P6 fitted on November 12, 1954. Both chassis and cab were built by Dennis and the 40-barrel (1,440gall) tank was built by Thompsons (Bilston) Ltd. Scammell coupling gear was fitted and Scammell also carried out the front mounting and fitted the rear axle, this being quite an early example of a chassisless trailer. That this must have been a relatively unusual addition to the fleet is suggested by the wealth of detail which was recorded about its measurements. A small sample is shown in the table.

	Tractor	Trailer	Combination
Overall length:	15ft 11in	18ft	27ft
Overall height:	7ft 5in	8ft 7in	9ft 3in
Overall width:	7ft 1in	7ft 3in	7ft 3in
Rear of cab to end of ramps:	5ft 11in		
Unladen weight:	2 ton 11cwt	2 ton 13cwt	5 ton 3cwt

(The slight anomaly in the additions results from rounding up the weights on the two components of the combination; the 'true' weight is the combination weight.)

An interesting comparison with the 1949 Dennis Horla is this Seddon which entered service on February 1, 1956. Only seven years of development have taken place but, in this time, a complete change has occurred in the appearance of heavy goods vehicles with styling being more identifiable with what is on the roads today. With an almost identical specification trailer to that behind the Horla the Perkins P6-engined Seddon differs in being shorter at 14ft 8in, higher at 8ft 2in and narrower at 7ft; it is also 4cwt (204kg) heavier at 2 ton 15cwt.

An object lesson to the unwary spotter, this almost identical Seddon – fleet number S136 – exhibits subtle differences from its fleet sister S105. This model has the Seddon De Luxe cab and a Perkins P6 engine which, the records proudly proclaim, is fitted with a thermostat (whatever next?)! Unladen weight of the tractor has been trimmed by a useful hundredweight (51kg) but the major differences lie with the tank. Of similar (40brl) capacity, this tank by Burnett & Rolfe Ltd is 1ft 7in shorter overall, this being compensated for by an increased width of 7ft 6in. These apparently modest changes enable a further 6cwt to be trimmed from the unladen weight – a useful feature in the Fifties when vehicle taxation depended upon the *un*laden weight of the vehicle rather than the total, or gross, weight which is used today.

This particular vessel entered service as an artic on October 28, 1957 having originally been mounted on a Crane drawbar trailer chassis. The conversion was carried out by Burnett & Rolfe and the Scammell coupling gear and rear axle were fitted by Cranes (Dereham) Ltd. Note that the slope of the tank is slightly less on this model than on either the Horla or the Seddon S105. The slope existed for several reasons: of necessity, the front end of the tank had to be high enough to clear the coupling apparatus, but at the same time it was desirable to keep the centre of gravity as low as possible to improve stability, especially when cornering. Most of these tankers discharged from the rear, by gravity, and a sloping tank ensured proper emptying, even if the vehicle itself was not absolutely level. Additionally, though, the steeper the slope, the smaller the surface area of the beer – a horizontal tank having the greatest surface area and a vertical one the smallest. Small surface area was desirable not only to prevent the beer giving up its CO_2 content but also to prevent 'fobbing' or frothing on the surface. There was an additional safety reason, too, because as already mentioned bulk liquids carriers experience 'surge' when the brakes are applied. These forces act horizontally and it was thought at the time that the slope assisted in dissipation of these forces, deflecting them into less hazardous directions. Had this been the case to a noticeable degree, a loss of braking effort would have been experienced as the driving wheels would have been lifted and traction would have been lost!

Whilst on the subject of tanks and tankers an experiment dating from April 1957 must be included which was not only successful in its own right but which, in modified form, plays a major part in the productivity equations of the Nineties. This was the demountable tank which weighed 3 ton 19cwt 1qr 14lb (3,969kg). Two could comfortably be carried on the larger vehicles – deck-length being the constraining factor rather than weight – and, as the photograph suggests, they were used mainly for exporting bulk beer, to Brussels in this case, for bottling. Unladen, these tanks weighed 14cwt 3qr (751kg) and their nominal capacity was 720 gallons (20brl or just under 3,300ltr). To maintain the beer in good condition a 'gas cover' was provided at a working pressure of 20psi; this involved simply filling the space at the top of the tank with carbon dioxide (CO_2) both to prevent the beer giving up its own CO_2 and so that any gas taken up by the movement of the beer's surface during transport was 'friendly' to the product.

These tanks, which were 6ft 8in high and 6ft 4in in diameter, were fitted with lifting lugs to enable them to be unloaded and, at both ends of their journey, a trolley was provided so that they could easily be moved about. On the opposite side of the tank to that shown was an access door for cleaning.

It could be claimed that these simple devices were the forerunners of several high-productivity ideas in use in the Nineties. Large capacity tanks, to International Standards Organization (ISO) dimensions are still used for conveying beers between the UK and mainland Europe, although most of the traffic is now in the opposite direction. Demountable tanks, of smaller capacity, are used by some brewers for delivering very large quantities to pubs – the demountable element being of great value in speeding-up turn-round at the depot so that vehicles are available for second and subsequent trips. With fixed tanks the vehicle is tied up whilst cleaning and filling processes are carried out.

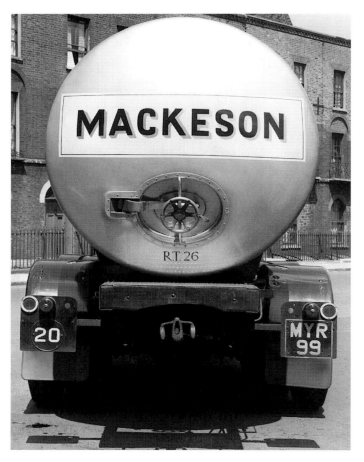

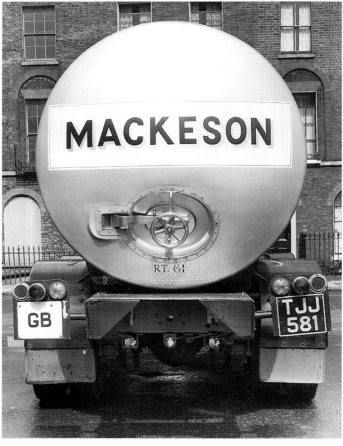

Some tail-ends. Above left: The back end of an 80-barrel (2,880gall) tank built by Burnett & Rolfe and mounted on a Marshalls of Cambridge-cabbed AEC Mark III 9.6-litre diesel eight-wheeler fitted for drawbar operation – note the drawbar hitch and the speed restriction to 20mph. This tanker entered service on November 3, 1952 with an unladen weight of 8 ton 15cwt.

Above: A similar tank for use on export runs, this one is not equipped for towing trailers. The tank is mounted on an Atkinson eight-wheeler which entered service on April 16, 1957, fitted with Clayton Dewandre automatic lubrication equipment – the first in the fleet to be so equipped. Automatic greasing of the chassis whilst the vehicle was in motion was another subtle productivity improvement since it enabled longer service intervals to be introduced. Left and below: Side and rear views of an interesting dual-compartment vessel manufactured by Burnett & Rolfe. Each compartment is of 20-barrels capacity, each having its own access door, filler and ladder. The coupling gear is, of course, of the Scammell automatic type but was mounted, as was the back axle, by Cranes of Dereham. Measuring 20ft 3in overall and 7ft 6in wide, this chassisless trailer entered service in early December 1957.

Above: A drawbar tank made by Burnett & Rolfe and mounted on a Cranes of Dereham chassis, this 40-barrel trailer entered service in April 1956 with an unladen weight of 2 ton 15cwt. Its overall length, including the tow-bar, was 21ft 2in and the chassis frame measured 17ft 8in. On the front of the chassis is an exhortation to drivers to 'secure (brake) hoses in the brackets provided to prevent kinking' – a dangerous occurrence as kinks could cut off the air supply to the brakes, rendering them ineffective. Below: A broadly similar tank showing the towing and braking gear.

CHAPTER SIX

Recent Times

History takes time to assess what is truly relevant and what is merely transitory and, as yet, insufficient years have passed to attempt a detailed assessment of anything more than the first two decades since 1960, even though some developments of the Eighties and early Nineties have been included here. Many factors – social, economic, political and technological – have contributed to vehicle design in the last 30 years, both within the brewery industry and in other spheres.

Amongst other things has emerged the rise of consumerism with its desire for wider choice and better quality. For the brewing industry, this has manifested itself most notably in the form of CAMRA, the Campaign for Real Ale. 'Real ale' is, in fact, exactly the same as the less well-liked (by CAMRA) keg beers, except that it is unfiltered and unpasteurized. 'Keg' beers were introduced in the early Sixties, Flowers Keg being the first, quickly followed by Watney's Red Barrel and, whilst not to everyone's taste, they did have the advantage that they travelled well, gave an absolutely consistent beer over a wide range of temperatures and other conditions, and required much less skill on the part of the publican in caring for and dispensing them. They also required a cask which could withstand gas pressure since they were dispensed by gas supplied from a separate cylinder of carbon dioxide. This meant having metal canisters as well as adding another product to the load which the dray had to distribute – the CO_2 gas cylinders.

The upsurge in interest in 'real ale' meant, to the distributor, that greater care had to be taken in handling the product and at maintaining temperatures within stricter bands. Offering the widest possible choice at the bar counter also often meant that regional beers had to be trunked the length and breadth of the country.

Brewers have witnessed a general decline in the amount of beer consumed, with lager taking an increased share of a diminishing spend. The market has also changed in other ways, with wines and ciders taking a larger share of consumers' expenditure. The increase in popularity of lagers has opened the door to imports, initially only from Europe but, latterly, increasingly from the United States. These changes have meant that deliveries have tended to consist of smaller quantities of a greater number of products and all this added variety has prompted the brewery distributor to integrate on to a single vehicle all the beers – whether in kegs, casks or bottles – as well as the wines, spirits, mineral waters and all the rest. In turn, this has had a pronounced effect on distribution operations in the brewery warehouse or depot, where loading methods and systems have had to change to accommodate the new needs of the customer.

Also within the marketplace, further acquisitions by the Big Six of small, regional brewery companies, and even greater concentration of brewing, packaging and distribution facilities, has seen the introduction of the mega-breweries, which brew in vast quantities and then transfer bulk beer to local racking plants where the product is racked into cans, bottles or kegs. It is then transferred again to a distribution depot, sometimes even via a regional distribution centre, so that the average pint can have travelled several hundred miles before it reaches the pub counter.

Of course, legislation has, as ever, played its part in influencing design, with sometimes sporadic and unco-ordinated changes to permissible weights and dimensions. This is discussed further in Chapter 7. Additionally, though, legislation has been enacted on such areas as Health and Safety at Work – ultimately influencing the weights which operatives are permitted to handle; even the Monopolies and Mergers Commission have investigated the industry and made proposals. Considerable changes have been seen in trade union attitudes, brought about partly by an enriched understanding of economic factors and partly

The Claymore 3 to 4-tonner Model MR7N was an unusual departure for Albion, whose products had, traditionally, been concentrated at rather heavier weights. The Claymore was introduced in 1954, not long after Albion's takeover by Leyland, when the Leyland-Albion-Scammell Group was formed, and it is rather odd that they were allowed to go ahead with the model so soon after the takeover. Presumably, plans were so far advanced that it was inevitable. Few of them were ever built, and later models – such as the one illustrated which dates from late 1963 – incorporated an under-floor four-cylinder diesel engine and overhead worm-drive rear axle, being much simplified compared with the earlier versions. The operator of this specimen was Rhymney Breweries, in South Wales, who were early pioneers with mechanized road transport of which many fascinating old photographs appear in 'Echoes of Rhymney' published by Starling Press in 1974.

This 1960 Cardiff-registered Thornycroft is an example of the last in a long line of vehicles dating back to 1934 bearing the model name 'Trusty'. Thornycroft were absorbed into the ACV group along with AEC and Maudslay and, whilst undoubtedly leaders in design and build quality, had begun to lag behind what the market was demanding. This model dates from the same year as the earliest of the TK Bedfords and from the era of the Ford Thames 4D, but it was more difficult to drive, having an old-fashioned constant-mesh gearbox compared with the part- synchromesh gearboxes available from the competition. This Thornycroft was in service with the brewer at the same time as the Albion Claymore illustrated on the previous page, and the pictures of the two vehicles may well have been taken on the same day.

by their diminished power as a result of falling membership and what is seen, by them, as hostile legislation. A corresponding change seems, however, to have taken place in managers' attitudes towards their workforces, with a new respect shown for the difficult and sometimes – especially in wet or very cold weather – unpleasant job which the dray-crews have to do, and a new willingness to work together for their mutual economic survival.

Undoubtedly, many other factors have also influenced the distribution environment and hence, ultimately, vehicle design. From the point of view of examining advancing vehicle productivity, the importance of the role which Information Technology – usually in the form of computers – has played cannot be overlooked. Computers play a major role in vehicle design, but are also now used routinely in traffic offices to calculate which loads should be placed on

which vehicles so as to minimize the amount of resource used. Most loading and delivery documentation is now computerized and we are on the threshold of a new era in which it will be commonplace for vehicles to have a data-processing computer in the cab: many vehicles are already fitted with communications equipment which can vary from a CB radio to a full cellphone and satellite tracking. The once-infamous tachograph – hailed at the time of its introduction as 'the spy in the cab', has been with us for many years and has proved its worth time out of hand, if only in providing an incontrovertible defence for drivers involved in accidents, but this too will surely be replaced by electronics yielding accurate driver and vehicle information, rather than just undigested data.

So, with all this activity, what has actually happened with vehicle design? The answer, of course, is a great deal and it is probably true to say that as much progress has been made in the last 30 or so years as in the entire period from the introduction of the internal combustion engine! To examine all the developments in detail is outside the scope of a book such as this – especially as concentration is placed on the story of how productivity has advanced. However, if the vehicle is considered as comprising four major components: chassis and cab, driveline (engine and transmission), running gear (wheels and suspension) and body, a reasonably methodical basis for review is established as significant progress has been made with productivity developments for each of these. Additionally, though, attention must be drawn to what has happened in the field of load unitization as this has had a profound effect on the subject matter.

Load unitization was a technique introduced on a large scale by the Americans during the Second World War in which loads were consolidated into units and handled as single entities rather than handling individual boxes of, for example, ammunition. The most obvious example of unitization is the pallet, on which large numbers of boxes can be stacked so that 50 or more cases can be handled at a single lift using a fork-lift truck. Another example of unitization which is frequently seen today, and almost taken for granted, is the International Standards Organization (ISO) shipping container which is equally suitable for sea, rail or road transport and is often used in the brewing industry for importing continental lagers in bulk (ISO) tanks.

It is, perhaps, no accident that so many of the photographs in this book are of Whitbread vehicles, in spite of strenuous attempts to find photographs from other brewers. The fact is that Whitbread have a history of being keen to develop new and better ideas in distribution and, from the early days of this century, have recorded their efforts on film. So it was Whitbread who, in the mid-Sixties, grasped the nettle and started rethinking the whole brewery distribution operation from scratch, resulting in giant strides being made in productivity development. Their competitors, Bass, however, were never far behind and indeed, in some fields, led the way.

The rethink revolved, essentially, around the adoption of

pallets. Conventional pallets, measuring about 40 x 44in (actually 1,000 x 1,200mm), were not quite right for kegs *or* crates. What was wanted was a new pallet which could accept, say, eight 11-gallon (50ltr) or five 22-gallon (100ltr) containers, representing something in the region of a half-ton weight, as well as being suitable for the various sizes of crate which existed. It was soon realized that the old-fashioned dozen-half-pint wooden crate was incompatible with modern-day thinking or palletized working so this needed to be changed too.

In the event, a plastic crate was designed which contained 15 half-pint bottles. Crates with identical or compatible base dimensions, holding bottle quantities other than a dozen, were also developed for pints and flagons. All the sizes had, of course, to be compatible with the vehicle which carried them, the dimensions of which were laid down by law, and these requirements were eventually met by designing a new pallet measuring 1,200mm – so that two could lie across the bed of a vehicle in the same way as a conventional ISO pallet – by 1,320mm.

Now to the vehicles themselves: chassis generally have become much lighter in their construction and weight as mathematics has been used instead of steel to ensure adequate strength. In the ultimate case, chassis have been dispensed with altogether, the strength residing in the construction of the body or trailer itself. As an interesting aside, the modern express bus has only a rudimentary chassis to hold the engine and wheels in place until the body, which contains all the strength, is fitted. This is not yet the case with heavy goods vehicles, but those with long memories will remember that it has been tried – by Jensen, in the Fifties.

The latest development for brewery vehicles is a step-frame chassis which gives an ultra-low deck height and good aerodynamics. The first of these appeared in the soft drinks industry as the spine-back, or Lamberhof design in which the chassis was effectively turned on its side. Ideal for soft-drinks, as not only could the pallets lean towards the centre line but a low deck-height was offered, it did not, however, prove so useful for brewers. This is because brewery deliveries often require that the load is worked across the vehicle from left to right and, with a large vertical spine in the way this was not possible. The answer was to construct a step in the frame which, however, introduced some interesting problems for the transmission designers as output from the engine needed to be turned through a sharp angle before running under the vehicle to the back wheels. One brewer tried overcoming this by the use of front-wheel drive, but this was not, at the time, a great success. It is interesting to see, however, that with more up-to-date technology, the idea has been revived, and Bass engineers have now developed a very promising-looking (and driving!) prototype. Chassis, then, have become lighter – allowing a greater payload within a given gross weight: and they have become lower – making the task of working from them less arduous, both of which are worthwhile improvements in the overall productivity equation.

Cabs are more comfortable, better ventilated, quieter and better instrumented than they were at the beginning of our review period so that drivers suffer less stress and have less physical hard work to do in actually driving. It could be claimed that this is more than compensated for by the reduction in the size of the average dray-crew (usually to two men) with the driver actively assisting with the load.

Engine technology has advanced fairly rapidly, today's engines having thermal efficiencies which were considered impossible not many years ago. Horsepower has increased from about 165–180bhp for the maximum gross weights

'Cellar tanking' was a popular way of delivering large quantities of beer to pubs at a single delivery and was a technique which was widely used in the north of England and some of the more industrial areas of the south, as well as in Scotland and the South Wales coal and steel areas, where beer consumption warranted it. This Atkinson four-wheeler, so evocative of the period, is equipped with very high-capacity (10brl) tanks and, right at the back, the 'permanently' fixed pumping apparatus. Registered in the West Riding of Yorkshire in 1967–8, this vehicle was used to service the larger outlets and working mens' clubs from the John Smith breweries at Barnsley and Tadcaster – home of the famous 'Taddy' ales. The motifs on the radiator grille have been slightly re-arranged; Atkinson's encircled 'A', which was introduced in 1937 and discontinued in the late Sixties, until consumer demand brought it back – albeit subtly altered – has been moved over to allow space for the (optional) silver 'Knight of the Road' badge – reminiscent of the old Atkinson steamers, as well as John Smith's magnet motif, advertising their Magnet ales.

In the early days, 'cellar tanking' required a special-purpose vehicle. To increase fleet flexibility as well as improving productivity by allowing more than one journey to be made each day, a system using demountable tanks, whose base dimensions were compatible with a brewery pallet, was introduced in the early Eighties. Right at the back of the vehicle can be seen the demountable service unit (DSU) which contained all the pumping, metering and hose equipment required to make deliveries. Each container holds five barrels (36gall) of beer and a similar-looking container is installed in the pub's cellar. Upon delivery, a hose is connected from the required tank on the vehicle to the DSU and from the DSU to the cellar tank. Pumping then begins into the bottom of the tank, which has usually been prepared by being thoroughly cleaned and inspected, before filling with CO_2 prior to delivery. This not only provides a gas-cover for the beer but also helps in the suppression of 'fob' or froth. Some brewers preferred to use a replaceable plastic bag which fitted inside the cellar tank and obviated the need for tank-cleaning and for charging with CO_2. The vehicle used is a normal dray from the everyday delivery fleet, as evidenced by the deck, which has been lowered by cutting-out to allow space for the wheels and whose raves (sides) are equipped for carrying CO_2 cylinders.

of 24–30 tons in 1960, to 290–350bhp for domestic work at 32–38 tonnes by the early Nineties. It is rare to find a vehicle now with horsepower anything like as low as the statutory minimum of 6bhp per ton!

Turbocharging, which uses the exhaust gases to drive a turbine which compresses the inlet air, is almost universal except on the very lightest vehicles and intercooling, which cools the compressed inlet air to make it even more dense, thus delivering more air per inlet stroke, is commonplace at the higher weights. The engines themselves are quieter and emit less unpleasant substances – diesel in any case emits almost no toxins compared with the environmentally unfriendly petrol – even unleaded petrol – engine. Experiments have been made in brewery fleets with fitting air-cooled engines made by Deutz, of Germany, to save the weight of the coolant required for a conventional engine.

Perhaps the gearbox and transmission has seen even greater advances than the engines. Six-speed gearboxes were the norm in the Sixties, when the engine's flexibility, ie useful rpm range, was greater than the technologically more advanced engines of today. The modern engine has a fairly narrow band of rpm, say 1,000 to 1,900 or even less, at which it operates at peak efficiency and maximum torque and, to enable it to stay within this range, more gears are provided, resulting in gearboxes with 10, 12, 16 or, as is the case with the top-weight Ivecos – 18 gears! On the face of it this is a retrograde step for productivity, but the payback comes with improved fuel consumption, better journey times and longer intervals between services. Computer-assisted gearchanges are offered by some manufacturers – notably Mercedes-Benz with their EPS gearboxes, and Scania, who also offer microprocessor-based engine management systems, fibre-optic instrumentation and self-diagnostic component checking.

Developments in the running-gear of vehicles are, perhaps, a little esoteric but, nevertheless, some interesting developments have occurred. New types of suspension involving air-bags or rubber have been introduced to the market in general and have, inevitably, found their way into brewery fleets. Rubber suspension has had a part to play in the general lowering of deck-heights to levels which formerly could only be achieved by cutting out areas of the deck for the wheels to run in, or by fitting wheelboxes. Air suspension has enabled fragile loads to be carried with fewer road-shocks being transmitted to the load and less damage being caused to the road surface. In the future new developments with carbon fibres, which have immense strength and very light weight, are likely to be seen.

Tyres have developed from the old crossply types to radials for commercial use, giving higher mileages and

Bedford introduced the TK range at the 1960 Motor Show in the weight range 3 to 7 tons. The range was later extended right up to the heavier KM at 16-tons GVW. The TK Bedford went on to become the mainstay of many brewers' fleets as well as being a general workhorse for many industries.

The photo shows a conventional four-wheeled diesel dray, fleet No B2763, and the registration mark indicates that it was registered in Portsmouth in 1970 at which time it was little changed in appearance since its introduction. Of interest is the palletized, mixed load of cases of beer, soft drinks, wines and spirits – a major step forward in productivity from the days when separate vehicles were used for each product. It would, though, be a rare event today to see wines and spirits carried on an *open* vehicle – especially on the hindmost pallet; how times have changed!

The drayman with the sack truck shows how columns of crates were carried as well as stacked on the pallet. Note the string round the top layer on the pallet to prevent sway. The wooden crates also show the degree to which the Big Six brewers integrated their operations from different regions. Portsmouth was Brickwoods country yet the crates are from Strong's (of Romsey) and Fremlin's (of Maidstone).

greater reliability. They have also improved to the extent that 'super-single' tyres can be fitted confidently on maximum-weight trailers, and low-profile tyres, once the prerogative of the sports car, can be fitted to delivery vehicles. Wheels, too, have played their part in productivity development, being constructed from light alloys, so reducing unladen weight.

It is possibly in the body department, though, that the most numerous, far-reaching and visible developments have taken place. In the early Sixties, a typical delivery dray was an open vehicle with some rudimentary method of load restraint. It would typically have had a 3 to 5-ton payload and would have been loaded by hand with occasional assistance from fork-lift trucks. Today, the massive increase in unitization of loads, mainly onto pallets, has entailed fundamental changes in the design of the vehicle to accommodate unitized loading. The modern dray is thus a closed vehicle, usually with side-curtains, and occasionally featuring some form of mechanical handling equipment. The most comprehensive handling equipment carried by a delivery dray was possibly the Kooi-Aap – a Dutch adaptation of a fork-lift truck which enabled it to 'climb' on to the rear of the vehicle for use, delivering in pallet quantities, at the point of delivery. At the other end of the scale is the ullage-crane, a simple pole and winch for

extracting part-full kegs from deep cellars, a requirement largely brought about by real ales having gone out of condition through age or mishandling.

In areas where beer was consumed in large quantities it was common to make semi-bulk deliveries by tanker. This requires a cellar-tank, usually of five barrels (180gall, or about 820ltr) capacity, which is fitted with apparatus for cleaning and for maintaining a good gas-cover for its contents. A hose is connected from the tanker to the cellar tank and the beer is then simply pumped and metered into the cellar. Clearly this requires good co-ordination of consumption, tank-cleaning and delivery but, whilst very productive when delivering, the system also had its drawbacks. It required a special-purpose vehicle which, upon returning empty to the depot, had to be cleaned before refilling such that it was often only possible for it to carry out one delivery round per day. This was overcome by making the tanks demountable so that they could be replaced by tanks of fresh beer in newly cleaned vessels for their second trip. But beer-drinking is seasonal and the vehicle, specially fitted with pumps, meters and plumbing, could be severely under-utilized during the winter months. The answer to this was to make the pumping and metering demountable as well so that a conventional vehicle could possibly be hired into the fleet during peak periods. It is good transport practice to minimize the fixed-cost elements of a fleet by setting permanent fleet strength at a figure near to the trough requirement, and to hire in for peaks. However, this is not always possible for brewers because the average vehicle available for hire neither has a strong enough floor for brewery work, nor is likely to be fitted with the necessary load security attachments.

Increases in the permitted gross weight of vehicles, together with further advances in mechanical handling technology, has had a marked effect on, particularly, the design of semi-trailers. Fork-lift trucks, capable of carrying four pallets of beer at one lift (two-high, side-by-side), have been developed to speed the loading of transfer vehicles and, for returning empty kegs to racking plants, enclosed trailers capable of carrying three layers of loaded pallets are now in use. Further to increase useful payload, several brewery groups use a specially adapted fork-lift truck to dispense with pallets altogether. This is done by locating the kegs with tines, instead of forks on the lift-truck, which engage direct on the rolling-ring of the kegs themselves. This way payload is not used up carrying useless pallets.

In 1960 transport and distribution managers were often seen as belonging to the back-end of an industrial process and were attributed little importance. The famous management writer, Peter Drucker, referred to distribution as 'management's dark continent' and certainly it was a part of the business which failed to attract very many men of calibre. How different it is today, having gained respectability as 'physical distribution management', later becoming seen as an essential element in 'supply chain management' and now attracting and retaining people of the highest calibre into the fashionable area of 'logistics', which recognizes that transport productivity is but one simple cog in the vast machine of materials management and that, if that cog is wrong, the business will function less efficiently as a result.

Most of the brewers used Bedford as the major supplier for their delivery fleet and this photo, taken in early 1978, gives an idea of just how standardized some fleets had become. Some of the vehicles here date from 1973 but it is difficult to observe which are the older and which are the more recent. The Bedford TK had many advantages: it was easy to drive, it was reliable and, because it was produced in vast numbers, most service mechanics knew how to deal with them. Spares were also relatively cheap – again reflecting the numbers produced – and there was a widely established dealer network.

Good relationships were enjoyed by the brewers with several vehicle manufacturers, but possibly none more so than with Bedford, who were always ready to experiment with different wheelbases, axle configurations, suspensions and so on – reflecting, no doubt, their strength both in the home and export markets. This photo shows a 1970 trial with a conventional six-wheeler enabling bigger payloads to be carried. With a mixed load, bottled beer was carried on pallets, right up against the headboard, and the kegs were carried further back on the platform – in this case on the slightly old-fashioned cradle pallets. In spite of careful route planning – which involved 'lefting' and 'righting' a load to avoid having to work across the vehicle when parked in a street – the old problem of axle overloading returned. Note that the dray crew consists of three men, a feature of brewery delivery for many years to come – and still the case in some areas.

Still with Bedford – and Whitbread – to illustrate the train of thought. In the Thirties, axle overloading problems had been overcome by adding an axle at the front to give the Chinese-six axle configuration. The same problem met with the same solution as this 1975-registered version shows. At this stage bottled beer was still predominantly in the old wooden crates, but some imported beers were appearing on the scene in plastic crates, albeit of the conventional dozen bottles.

This photo shows mechanical handling in use for loading around 38 crates at one lift. Beneath the bed of the vehicle can be seen steel racks for carrying the carbon dioxide cylinders needed for dispensing the new-fangled keg beer and the body-type itself is a newcomer to the scene. This is a Boalloy Tautliner curtain-sided vehicle which gave excellent load retention as well as protection. The curtains, having tensioners or straps, which extended from the cant rail to the rave underneath which they were buckled, were capable of supporting a load which had shifted whilst in transit. There was, of course, no legislating for the misguided drayman who, realizing his load had moved, opened the curtain to see what was going on!

Another approach to bodywork for beer delivery is this unusual dropside, semi-stake-sided dray based at Watney's Mortlake brewery. Apart from a deck-height so low that it needed wheel-boxes cutting out, it is difficult to see what advantages this could possibly have had. What appears to be a slightly modified LAD cab, together with the fleet number AC 210, suggest that the vehicle may have been an Albion for about 12 to 14-tons gross working. If so, that would date the photo to the Sixties when Watney's competitors were already experimenting with load restraining curtain-siders. This attempt, in having a roof to protect both the product and the dray crew, is a step better than the 'boxing-ring' vehicles, which used stanchions and chains, and which date from earlier in the Sixties. Watney's vehicles were always neatly turned out with the red wheels and the famous Red Barrel setting off the dark green bodywork very attractively. Watney's share with Whitbread the honour of wearing the Royal Warrant as a part of their livery.

The Sixties could be called the decade of mergers and acquisitions as far as the British commercial vehicle industry is concerned. This 1966 Leyland Super Comet, produced from about 1961 by the Leyland-Albion-Scammell group, which became the British Leyland Motor Corporation, which in turn later became British Leyland, is adorned with an 'LAD' cab. The LAD cab was so-called because it shared many of its pressed-steel panels with Albion models (the Clydesdale four-wheelers and Riever six-wheelers) as well as Dodge middleweights built at Kew. The initials stood for Leyland, Albion, Dodge and, with minor modifications, became the standard cab for the Leyland range. This Super Comet was fitted with Leyland's 400 model diesel engine, the numerals indicating the engine's cubic capacity in Imperial units – cubic inches, a feature more common in the United States than in Europe where, since the Twenties, engine sizes have been measured in litres or cubic centimetres (1,000cc = 1 litre).

Before any new ideas could be let loose on the road they had to be rigorously tested. Various facilities were used for these tests depending upon what was required but, frequently, an old aerodrome sufficed. Later, when testing became more scientific than just trying to see whether the load would stay on or the vehicle would turn over when cornering, or that the steering, suspension or brakes were good enough for the job, the test facilities of the Motor Industry Research Association (MIRA) at Nuneaton were used.

The effectiveness of the Tautliner curtain is seen to good effect in these photos in which the artic trailer is being tested with a load made up of pallets of kegs, stacked three-high.

Haulage and distribution by third-party contractors is a prominent part of today's brewery distribution scene, but it is new only in the extent to which it is now used. There have always been times when hauliers were used for specific jobs, particularly 'one-way' movements, where the haulier can provide a return load in the opposite direction. In 1969, from when this ERF 'A' Series tractor unit with LV cab styling dates, many hauliers and most drivers would have loved to own a unit such as this. Suspension had been significantly updated from previous models, sound insulation in the cab made the task of driving easier and less stressful and, of course, there was the legendary Gardner engine with 180bhp on offer. At 28 tons this represented nearly 6½bhp per ton – only just above what is now the statutory minimum. Units like this would typically have hauled loads of 'finished goods' or packaged (ie bottled) beer from the Northern breweries to depots in the Midlands and South. Beer crates would have been palletized and the whole load neatly roped and sheeted – a skill which is fast disappearing from the haulage scene, largely due to the introduction of curtain-sided vehicles.

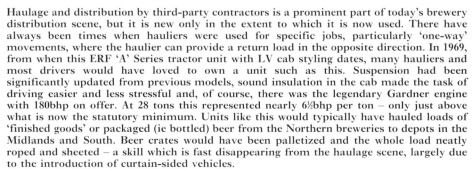

Two more examples of the lengths to which brewers go to ensure that their vehicles are stable and that they can cause no danger to the public. The photos were taken at the Motor Industry Research Association's test track at Nuneaton during Bass' routine testing of load-shift characteristics with a Boalloy Tautliner and a normal sheeted load. On the Tautliner, note how the cantrail at the top of the curtain is distorted with the weight which it is carrying as the load's centre of gravity has shifted. Also clearly visible is the protective gear which the specially qualified MIRA test drivers have to wear – just in case there is a failure. The sheeted load is on the point of balance with the steel shoe on the outrigger rubbing against the ground and sending up a shower of sparks, but preventing the actual roll-over. The steel shoe on the outrigger is made from mild steel, 40mm (about 1½in) thick, and wears out completely in three test sessions! Attached to the outrigger and to the underside of the vehicle are various measuring devices, with instruments and electronic readouts in the cab to measure lateral acceleration, centrifugal forces and so on. The method of testing involves driving the vehicle in a circle of measured radius at steadily increasing speeds. Once a series of measurements has been obtained for one radius and set of speeds, the radius is tightened and a new, smaller radius is driven. Only by carrying out these stringent tests can operators be sure that their vehicles pose the smallest possible risk to the safety of pedestrians and other road users.

When the trials on the 33m roll-over track have been completed satisfactorily, there is still a further stage of testing to go through. This involves driving the vehicle at various speeds and with various load configurations in what are more like real road-going conditions. This involves both high and low-speed driving, reversing and 'snaking'. A vehicle is said to 'snake' when, for example, it has to swerve violently as it would if a child ran out in front of it. Snaking can be experienced at a much lower speed when traversing a single – or even a succession of – mini-roundabouts or when manoeuvring in a tight yard. It is during this final stage of testing, which is carried out by several different drivers, each performing a predetermined number of circuits, that things – very occasionally – go wrong. This Bedford TM, *on loan* (!) from United Service Garages, in Portsmouth, is one that didn't make it on this occasion when too much speed was used for the amount of lock applied. Fortunately, no-one was hurt, but it was definitely a case of 'back to the drawing-board' for the combination as a whole.

Drawbar trailers offer several advantages in operation; in effect – and especially if used in conjunction with a properly engineered demountable system – the operator gets two loads for the price of one. For example, in areas which are a long way from the depot, a demount and drawbar unit can haul both 'waggon and drag' to the area; leave the trailer whilst delivering the load on the waggon; return and swap bodies; then deliver the trailer's load. Exceptionally, this can be accomplished in a single day – where the so-called 'stem' mileage is relatively low – but even if not there is a saving of one return trunking leg. One of the disadvantages which the conventional (ie wheel at each corner) drawbar trailer has is that it is difficult to reverse since it articulates at the coupling *and* at the axle turntable. To overcome this many drawbar waggons are fitted with a coupling and the associated brake-air hoses at the front so that the trailer can be nosed into position, as illustrated in this photograph. Note that the trailer is marked as being 18m in length; this applies to the entire rig and was the absolute legal maximum at the time.

An Atkinson in Watney's livery joins the fleet to operate at 24-tons gross combination weight. The cab is non-standard and may have been specified to accept a larger-than-normal engine. Motor Panels Ltd were often called upon to do this sort of work although it was probably more common on Fodens – a comparative rarity in brewery fleets in modern times. Note the handwheel for winding on the trailer brake and also the generally crude design of the landing gear. Wheels on landing legs are reminiscent of the days of the Scammell automatic coupling when the trailer could sometimes move back a few inches. Modern landing gear still occasionally features wheels but the 'elephant's foot' type is more common except on trailers which have air suspension. For air-suspended trailers it is usual to have a curved foot, like a sector of a very much larger wheel. This is because if a semi-trailer is left standing and air leaks from the suspension there will be movement along the length of the deck which would snap the legs unless they had the freedom to move forward a little. The effect can be observed when the sector has ridden up the back of the leg giving the effect of a (38-tonne) ballet dancer standing on tip-toes!

A late example of the long-running Ford D Series, of which many thousands were operated in the UK and overseas. The Ford D was a robust and simple-to-drive truck, relatively easy to maintain and with good spare parts availability and pricing, yet it never became a forerunner in the brewery industry, almost always being eclipsed by its rival the Bedford TK series. The predilection for Bedfords may date back to the immediate postwar period when many ex-servicemen found jobs as drivers, or draymen, in the industry, bringing with them the experience and reputation of the 250,000 odd Bedfords which formed the backbone of the army's transport fleet. The Ford Model D in the photo is the 14-tonner with the 140bhp engine and Custom cab and Boalloy Localiner bodywork. Custom cabs, apart from enjoying one or two optional extras, had from the brewers' point of view the advantage of having good seating for a crew of three. Some brewers, notably in London, even managed to squeeze a crew of four into this cab, but that was in the days when productivity was of less concern than it is today!

Demountable bodies were popular with some brewery groups but not with others. During the Eighties, the Grand Metropolitan group and, to a lesser extent, Scottish and Newcastle breweries, tried a number of ideas and combinations of drawbar and demountable systems with varying degrees of success whilst Bass and Whitbread concentrated their efforts in the areas of lower deck-heights, larger-capacity trunkers and cellar tanking. They all had a common desire to improve the productivity of their transport and delivery operations. Illustrated is a larger-capacity-than-usual Scania demountable for operation at around 24 tonnes gross. The body shown, in the livery of Grand Met subsidiary Ushers of Trowbridge, appears to be of the standard box variety rather than the more frequently encountered curtain-sider, suggesting its use for distribution of wines and spirits, boxvans being rather less vulnerable from the security viewpoint. The disadvantage with such a body for brewers is that boxvans usually require a loading dock as they are loaded across the tail, and many brewery depots do not possess such a luxury. One way round this, of course, is to fit a tail-lift but this is relatively slow – and noisy, especially if night operations are envisaged – so is not a method favoured by brewery transport engineers.

Evidence that the 1980 trials – to obtain three-high loading of pallets on transfer vehicles – was nothing new is in the form of this Scammell Trunker II operated by Threlfall's Brewery in the Liverpool and Birkenhead areas. The twin-steer tractor unit had an unladen weight of 6 ton 2cwt 2qr (6,236kg) enabling it to tackle a 42-pallet, mixed load of empty stainless steel and aluminium 11-gallon (50ltr) containers. The trailer is a standard flatbed, not designed specifically for this type of load, so 'dunnage' – in the form of empty pallets stacked against the headboard – is needed to ensure that the load centre is in the correct position in relation to the axles and kingpin to avoid illegal overloading. The cab is the famous 'Scammell cheese-grater', the 'Michellotti master-piece' made from glassfibre and very popular in other industries on the eight-wheeled Routeman chassis.

This Bedford TM 3400, specially fitted out with aluminium bumper and fuel tank – to 'add lightness' – is one of a batch of seven supplied to Bass for operation out of their Cape Hill brewery. In Bedford's vehicle range the TM replaced the earlier KM 32-tonners which never caught on as (then) maximum weight vehicles, possibly because Bedford had not yet established a reputation at these higher weights. Even the TM, though, which had several quite advanced features including a Detroit Diesel two-stroke engine and was designed specifically for working at 32 tons and above, never became a favourite with fleet operators within or outside the brewing industry. It required a change of driving habit for many drivers, as the two-stroke engine required revs to be kept high, unlike most diesels where the greatest torque is experienced at low revs. As a result they turned in poor fuel efficiency figures and were reputed to be unreliable. In the Bass fleet the TMs replaced Guy 'Big J4T' tractor units whose unladen weight was only 5 ton 10cwt (5,600kg). The Big J4Ts were decidedly 'old-technology' even at the time, having noisy, draughty cabs, naturally aspirated engines and tricky gearboxes. The designation J4T is of interest: the Big J range covered most of the heavyweight configurations, Big J8s and Big J6s being eight and six-wheelers respectively. The addition of a 'T' denoted that the vehicle was a tractor unit. The 'J' stood for Jaguar who had acquired the company and for whom this range was their first entry into HGV production. In turn, the Guys had replaced the Scammell Handyman which had, initially Rolls-Royce Eagle I engines, superseded by Rolls-Royce Eagle IIs, then by the Cummins 14-litre unit and finally – in the Bass fleet – by Rolls-Royce Eagle IIIs. Bass did not introduce the Crusader to follow the Handyman because it was too heavy, the unladen weight of the Handyman varying from under 5 tons to about 5 ton 7cwt depending upon which engine was fitted.

Paused during a day's testing at MIRA, these two vehicles remind us that compatibility of pallets, crates and kegs must extend across both the delivery and the trunk vehicle – and with production facilities at the brewery.

The Ford Cargo 16-tonner in the picture is a prototype, specially fitted with rubber suspension – in an attempt to lower the deck-height as far as possible without significantly changing the technology of the vehicle itself. It also has a Deutz air-cooled engine – to save the weight of the coolant required with water-cooled engines – a combination which demonstrates the lengths to which engineers will go to develop the ideal vehicle.

The Volvo F12 trunker is seen coupled to a tri-axle trailer to experiment with gross weights in excess of the legal limit of 32 tons. This was in anticipation of legislation changing to a higher permissible maximum weight, but both operators and manufacturers were kept in the dark about what the new legislation would allow. The popular view at the time (1982, when this photo was taken) was that the new weight would be 34–36 tons on five axles. The result was that when the announcement was made declaring 38 tonnes to be the limit, British manufacturers were not ready and the floodgates were opened to European producers who had been supplying continental operators at these weights for years.

The Ford D-series was at the time Ford's most significant ever introduction to the heavy goods vehicle market. Many thousands were sold to every kind of industry, including brewers and, perhaps because they rapidly became so commonplace, few photographs seem to have been taken of them. This photo is a slight intruder because it is not a dray nor even a beer tanker. However, it does illustrate this immensely popular vehicle in its Custom Cab guise. Originally the D800, for 16-tons GVW working or up to 24 tons as a tractor unit, the model designation was later changed to D 1614 for the top weight rigid and to D 1624 for the artic. The 16 represented the maximum gross weight for the chassis and the 14 and the 24 represented 140bhp and 240bhp respectively, a form of model designation which has now been adopted by several manufacturers. The vehicle illustrated was registered in Glasgow in 1967, when this photo was taken, and was employed transporting bulk spirit to bottling plants.

Moves towards metrication, in the form of 50 and 100-litre kegs (holding 11gall and 22gall respectively), together with a complete rethink about packaging dimensions generally, resulted in a great advance in distribution productivity for one brewer. A new, specially designed pallet, which was compatible not only with the new metric kegs and a newly designed range of bottle cases, but with both the transfer and the delivery vehicle and even, though to a lesser extent, the mechanical handling equipment used at the brewery and the depots, was central to the rethink. The diagram shows how the pallet catered for eight 11-gallon containers or five at 22 gallons. A slightly less effective fit was obtained by four of the old, traditional (36gall) barrels or by five (18gall) kilderkins – or 'kils' – but these generally are being phased out in favour of the metric containers. *Cases* of bottled beer are usually stacked, on brewery pallets, in a different manner from what is common in other industries. Usually, the layers of cases are 'tied', meaning that alternate layers have the stacking pattern reversed, so that the load becomes much like a single solid entity. This is unsatisfactory for brewery deliveries as, frequently, a 'column' of cases is delivered at one drop, so there is no tying (or 'lacing' as it is sometimes called). Pallets made up of individual columns have a tendency to sway, so it is common practice to 'string' round the top, or next to top, layer, which has the effect of preventing the load from starting to move.

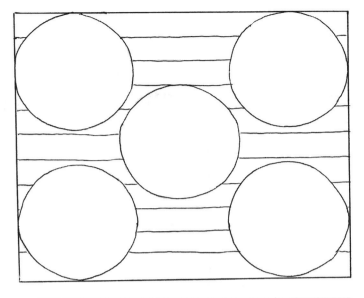

In 1990, Hartlepool-based Brent Walker Brewing put a fleet of seven of these Leyland DAF FAS 2300 HT models into service to deliver beer all over the north of England. In common with most posed publicity shots, headlights are on full-beam – presumably to show that they *do* work! This is a more or less conventional dray – albeit with an engine which is larger than usual for brewery application to give it the added power for long and hilly journeys – with no special efforts having been made to keep the deck-height particularly low. It is, in fact, a reliable, well-proven, off-the-shelf vehicle fitted with the brewery-standard side curtains. Note, in the warehouse, the different pallet configurations from different brewers: five to a pallet for the 'kils' and '22s', behind the vehicle and eight to a pallet for the '11s' on the driver's offside; also cradle pallets which hold four kegs on their sides; note also the 'column-stacking' of crates on the pallets and how well they fit the outside pallet dimension.

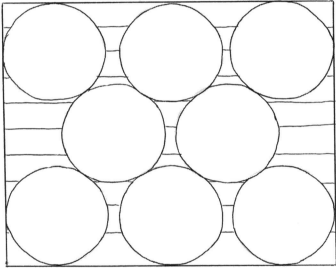

Capable of one-man operation was the Bedford KM with the Kooi-Aap attachment. The Kooi-Aap is a Dutch adaptation of a more-or-less conventional fork-lift truck, and consists of a portable device which can handle pallets on and off the vehicle. Whilst being very simple to operate, the 'Kooi' made steering very light on the earlier prototype vehicles on which it was tried, particularly when the vehicle was empty, as it almost lifted the front wheels off the ground. The problem was solved by further adaptations to the lift-truck and by altering the vehicle's body position in relation to the wheelbase. At its most productive when used in conjunction with a drawbar trailer, this machine enabled one man to operate in the remoter parts of a depot's territory on his own without having to return to base for a second load.

A study in concentration as the author attempts to find out, in Friesland, North Holland, how easy the Kooi-Aap was to use. Standing behind him is Dirk Kooi, the designer, and in the background can just be seen Alec Rendall, the project manager who worked on the development of the Kooi for brewery use.

Development of vehicles has become very sophisticated and now extends beyond vehicles which are required simply for the delivery operation into the domain of other vehicles required to support the whole brewing operation. This photograph, from 1985, shows a trailer for carrying bulk malt (processed barley for brewing) which was developed not just for the job it was required to do, but also specifically for the tractor unit with which it was to be used. The objective given to the Bass development engineers was: 'to specify and build a prototype Bulk Grain Trailer compatible for use with Volvo F.10-20 Tractor Units for operation at 38-tonne GTW (gross *train* weight) with top loading, central gravity discharge and sufficient capacity for a 25-tonne payload (1,765cu ft) within UK legal weight limits.' Additionally, they were required to carry out weight, loading and discharge trials, MIRA stability trials, and road-testing to ensure that the trailer met the various requirements of different departments within the company. The project resulted in a report and specification running to *over 50 pages* covering all aspects of design and operation. This detailed specification was turned into a reality by Don-Bur trailers. Note the use of the term gross *train* weight, which is sometimes used instead of gross *combination* weight when describing artics, although it is more usually confined to cases where separate, rather than semi-trailers are concerned.

Forerunner to the Kooi-Aap, and further proof if any was necessary that 'there's nothing new', is this contraption manufactured by Schildkrote. The photograph is undated but other vehicles present suggest the date as being in the late Fifties or early Sixties; there are no surviving records to tell us anything about this or even to say whether it was ever used in practice. Its appearance suggests battery power and the fact that the load deck has had to be cut out to place the weight nearer the rear axle suggests that this was a heavy beast. However, the method of raising and lowering the device on and off the vehicle seems to be identical to that used on the Kooi-Aap some 20 years later. This process entailed slotting the lifting forks into two 'pockets' at the back of the vehicle, and then using the controls set to *lower*. Since it could not in fact 'lower' the vehicle any further, this had the effect of *raising* the lift-truck on to the vehicle, suspended by its forks. The arrangements for securing the Kooi-Aap are more rigorous than those on the Schildkrote truck appear to be, these seeming to consist only of a bar across the aperture, secured by two snibs.

Nearly 30 years before the Volvo grain-trailer combination, bulk grains were hauled in vehicles like this 9.6-litre AEC diesel-engined Atkinson which entered service in June 1958. With power-assisted steering, a cab by Marshalls of Cambridge and a body by Sparshatts – tipped by B&E tipping gear – this was quite an advanced vehicle for its day. The 1,000cu ft payload weighed 15 tons within a gross weight of 24 ton 9cwt 3qr, (15,293kg and 24,933kg respectively) giving a very respectable gross to tare ratio of 2.58:1. This compares quite favourably with the more recent figures obtained with the Volvo combination which achieved a ratio of 2.92:1, thus showing a 13% improvement and, of course, at a much higher weight, payload being a full 10 tonnes more! Other interesting comparisons are:

	1958 Atkinson	1985 Volvo
Overall length	28ft 8in	45ft 2in
Overall height	11ft 10in	12ft 9in
Overall height – tipped	20ft 3in	
Overall width	8ft	8ft 2in
Body length	20ft 9in	36ft
Body height	6ft 7in	8ft 6in

One of the first chassis to be converted to the step-frame specification, which allowed ultra-low deck-heights for brewery use, was a DAF 2100, in the early Eighties. Many lessons were learned on this prototype, including how to transmit drive to the rear wheels through some very sharp angles for the propshaft. The design had a strong appeal to many brewery operators, particularly because of the low platform height which was obtainable without having the encumbrance of a central spine as was the case with the Lamberhof 'spine-back' designs which are quite common – and entirely acceptable – in soft-drinks work. Many chassis manufacturers eventually adopted the idea and the photograph shows a 1988 ERF E6 rigid with Boalloy Linkliner bodywork. The drayman, using his bump-bag, is clearly exerting less effort unloading from this height than he would using a similar technique from a higher deck. However, skilled draymen rarely lifted or manoeuvred casks themselves, always letting the load do the work, either by using gravity or by rolling it along the ground. The lower deck-height, though, is a much safer method of handling overall and also has a small payback in improved fuel consumption due to the improved aerodynamics. ERFs rarely featured in brewery delivery fleets, but with the introduction of the E-series with their low unladen weight and Cummins B-series 6-litre engines they provide an ideal tool for the brewery distributor.

These photos, taken before a body was fitted, show how a dropframe chassis is constructed. The conversion of a Bedford TL 16-ton chassis was carried out for Bass Brewers by Chassis Developments Ltd of Leighton Buzzard, and the amount of additional strengthening required, once a chassis deviates from a straight line, can clearly be seen. The inset photos show (left) the details of the step-down behind the cab with the engineering required to make the propshaft horizontal and (right) of the suspension, which was by Neway Suspensions, together with the brakes and final-drive, which are all neatly encapsulated in the wheelbox arrangement over the rear axle. Many attempts were made by various operators and manufacturers to keep deck heights as low as possible, some being much less successful than others. For some reason, this particular version did not go into line production, remaining as a test-bed prototype. Others which did not catch on at the time include the 'Titan' *portal frame* design in which the chassis stepped *up* to go over the top of the body. This required front-wheel drive and special bodies which could be preloaded at the depot. A fork-lift truck would push the body into position under the portal frame so that it could hang there, using a device similar to the ISO twist-locks used on shipping containers to keep it in place. A version of this did, in fact, go into service with Coca-Cola in Germany, but the unladen weight – with all the steel required to construct the portal – was against it and the design was never a real success, even though the deck-height could be reduced to about 100mm.

Burton-upon-Trent is very much a brewing town and it is reputed that by the year 1600 there were already some 46 licensed victuallers in business there. Today the major brewers are Bass, Marstons and Ind Coope, but it is not so long ago that there were many more. Burton itself used to have its own railway network actually *within the town* and the main streets were adorned with railway lines in a system which connected to the main rail system so both internal transport and local delivery as well as long-distance distribution in large quantities was easily catered for. In the Bass museum in Burton is a working model of the old town and its rail system, said to be the largest working railway model in Europe – and well worth a visit! The photo shows one of the last of the railway motive units to be used by Bass but, sadly, few details of its specification seem to have survived. The locomotive was built by Sentinel – the same people who used to build the road-going steam lorries – and, in this relatively recent photo, it appears that it is about to be loaded on to a low-loader.

These rather special demountable bodies operated by Grand Met's Phoenix Brewery, were produced by Ray Smith Demountables and are fitted on to Dodge Commando 100G16C chassis. This simple statement conceals the fact that some clever engineering had taken place to arrive at this very advanced concept which, surprisingly, did not catch on to the extent that it was copied by other brewers. The main photograph shows just how clever this was as a demountable, being hydraulically raised to clear the chassis yet snuggling down to provide a very low-profile dray in travelling and working mode. Apart from that, the vehicle is quite standard, even providing a flat working deck within the dray. The curtain sides are Don-Bur Slide-a-Side.

Rarely seen in brewery fleets is the Mercedes-Benz range of vehicles, even though there are models available from 3 to 38 tonnes (and above, but not for UK working!). This model, operating for Courage and liveried for Foster's lager, is the Mercedes-Benz 1617, the model number denoting that it is for 16-tonnes gross working and is fitted with a 170bhp engine. Both figures are only approximations, the 16 tonnes actually being 16.29 tonnes (16 tons) and the 170 being slightly less on early models and about 175 on later ones. Mercedes vehicles were sometimes known as 'the bosses' truck' because of their good fuel consumption, long maintenance intervals and general longevity, but low standards of driver comfort with a not-very-comfortable seat, unergonomic gearchange and noisy cab. The latest models, however, overcome these criticisms and even offer, on the heavier tractor units, 'EPS', the electronic power-shift gearchange. Compare the task of the drayman in this picture with that involved with purpose-built drays with low decks: here he is not only standing on tip-toe, but is having to stretch to reach his load! The carbon dioxide cylinders, with their yellow collars, are clearly visible in what has become the conventional storage place for them – beneath the body: on some vehicle designs they are concealed by the closed curtain. The yellow collar indicates that the cylinders are owned by the Courage group, each of the major brewers having their own distinctive colour: red for Watneys (Grand Met); orange for Allied Breweries and blue for Whitbread; other brewers shared cylinders with black collars.

A typical driver's cab of the early Sixties, this photo of a Leyland Vista Vue cab specially equipped for the brewing industry by having seating for a three-man crew shows just how crude driving conditions were at the time. This vehicle would have been for about 5 or 6-tons payload and almost certainly would not have been equipped with power-assisted steering. Instrumentation is the basic minimum of a speedometer – this was before the days of tachographs! – within the bezel of which would have been a fuel gauge and possibly a coolant temperature gauge. Ignition, oil-pressure and turn indicator tell-tales would have been by coloured lamps on the dash. The gearbox was a simple four or five-speed unit and the handbrake on this model was beside the seat at the driver's right hand. Alternative positions adopted by some manufacturers included down between the seats and, on the Commer 'Walk Thru', on the steering column.

The existence of the spare key still on the key-ring suggests that this photograph was taken before the vehicle went into service, as does the generally clean and new condition of the seats and carpet.

A pair of conventional drays of the late Eighties and early Nineties on Seddon Atkinson 201 chassis, with turbocharged and intercooled engines for maximum output and economy. Both have similar bodywork of the type which has become almost a standard for brewery and a lot of other distribution work, being one or other form of side curtain. This particular version is the Boalloy Localiner, distinguishable by the first and last half metre or so each side being in the form of a sliding door, compared with the Tautliner in which the whole length of the curtain is flexible and can be removed and swung aside. The clean and attractive appearance of these drays is due partly to the general design of the vehicle but, more prominently, to the excellent livery which has been applied and which follows cleanly through from cab to bodyside. This is a clever piece of marketing by John Smith who obviously recognize the benefits of a mobile advertising hoarding which is kept clean and attractive. They are also so much less obtrusive when kept in this condition – a major factor with a public which many believe is hostile to the heavy goods vehicle!

A similar view, taken from the nearside door of a 1991 AWD-Bedford 17-tonner. At first glance there is not much difference from the Sixties Leyland but there are, in fact, several important differences, most of which are ergonomic. The rake of the steering wheel is more comfortable; the gearchange lever has a shorter travel and is in a position in which the hand falls naturally onto it; the seats are more comfortable and many of the hand controls are grouped around the steering column for ease of operation. Instrumentation is slightly more comprehensive – but still relies to a large extent on warning lights – and, of course, a tachograph is included where the speedometer used to be. All-round vision is improved and the side windows have a cut-out at the lower front edge to allow a better view of what is happening in a notorious blind-spot, invariably populated by children, other pedestrians or cyclists! Note also the very large rear-view mirror on the door post which compares with the typical, 5in diameter circle of mirror fitted in the late Fifties.

David J B Brown's company AWD Ltd stepped in to rescue the old-established firm of Bedford when General Motors ceased to support their loss-making activity in the UK. With a relatively minor facelift from the previous Bedford TL range the AWD-Bedford attempted to carve its own niche in the brewing trade. Fitted with the 160bhp Perkins Phaser diesel engine, which was also available as a 180bhp option, the AWDs somehow still retained the familiar sound of the old TK/TL range of well-loved vehicles. The Foster's example illustrated, operated by Courage Breweries, has a stake-sided body with removable bars to aid unloading. Registered in Maidstone in 1989, this TL 13-16 is for gross weight operation at 13-tonnes GVW. Its load consisted, unusually in 1989, of barrels (36gall) and '22s' (22-gallon or 100-litre kegs). AWD became part of the Marshalls Group in 1992.

A posed publicity shot with number-plates indicating the model designation TL 18-16, this AWD went into operation at the Mansfield brewery making deliveries to public houses. These 'urban artics' are much favoured in the north of England; less so, it would seem, in the south – except, perhaps by the Bass group. They can have several advantages over a rigid vehicle, being 'flexible' enough to manoeuvre into difficult yards with their vastly improved turning circle. They also have a low deck-height on a long and level deck which aids unloading, and 'axle tolerance' is greater than a rigid vehicle which is helpful with diminishing loads. 'Axle tolerance' can best be explained for a rigid vehicle: suppose the vehicle has a maximum permissible gross weight of 15 tonnes; its axles might be rated at 6 tonnes for the front axle and 10 tonnes for the rear – a total of 16 tonnes, thus giving a tolerance of 1 tonne. The urban artic, with two axles at the front end of the platform, clearly scores here.

This vehicle would normally carry a crew of two men and the load would normally consist of mixed kegs and cases (note the sack truck, for use with cases, stowed beneath the rave on the nearside). Some brewers or brewery distributors also carry wines and spirits as well as soft drinks and minerals on the same load. That this practice is not universal only indicates that for some the gains in transport productivity, and hence savings, are outweighed by the inconveniences on the warehousing side of the operation. Increasingly, distributors are applying the principles of logistics to their operations and trading off additional costs in one part of the operation to gain larger savings in another part.

The word Tautliner has become a generic term for load-restraining, curtain-sided, bodywork. Shown here is a selection of publicity photographs of the standard Tautliner body on a variety of chassis. Boalloy were the first manufacturers of curtain-sided vehicles to offer load restraint within the curtain as distinct from simply load protection. This is achieved by the tensioners, or straps, running from top to bottom of the curtain, making a flexible but strong connection between the pelmet and the rave of the body. Shepherd Neame and McEwans have opted for an eight-strap version whilst Webster's, who may have different operating procedures or loading parameters, have chosen a 12-strap curtain for added strength.

A handsome example from the top of the weight range, this 400bhp Leyland DAF FTG 95.400 is operated by Robson Road Haulage on their Holsten contract which involves deliveries of palletized bottled beer to breweries throughout the UK. With a twin-steer tractor and a tri-axle trailer on air-suspension, this outfit is well-equipped not only for maximum weight operation but also to take advantage of Road Fund Licence concessions for vehicles which spread their load over a larger number of axles. In 1993, the duty rate for a *two-axle* tractor unit used with 'any' semi-trailer (ie having one, two or three axles) was £3,100 per annum but for a *three-axle* tractor unit, *only* used with a *three-axle* semi-trailer, the duty was a mere(!) £1,240 per annum, a saving of 60%. As ever, though, every silver lining has its cloud, and the tax saving comes at the penalty of a higher tare weight and consequent smaller payload compared with a two-axle tractor. The operator must perform his own trade-off calculations.

Boalloy's Localiner body on a Bedford TL 1630 for Scottish and Newcastle Breweries, liveried for McEwans, in 1985, and on an urban artic trailer for Bass in 1988. In the early days of curtain-siders only a limited selection of base colours was available for curtains and great difficulty was experienced in applying livery to them. One ingenious way of painting complex logos was to park the vehicle in a darkened paint shop and, using a 35mm slide projector, to project the image on to the side of the tightly stretched curtain. The signwriter then simply painted round what was on the 'screen'! These photographs clearly demonstrate how the situation has changed with liveries on curtain-siders now being as complex and attractive as any to be seen.

A selection of Tautliners on maximum-weight trailers of various makes. These are for palletized loads of either bottled or kegged beer and would normally be confined to reasonably long-distance work. The clear advantage of a curtain-sided vehicle is the fact that it can be unloaded from the sides and is not, therefore, tied to the need for a loading dock. Moreover, both sides can be unloaded at once so that very fast turn-round times can be achieved. The ultimate turn-round for vehicles of this size remains the 'drop and pick up' system, in which a loaded trailer is exchanged for an empty one. This is not always possible, though, particularly in cases where more than one delivery must be made from the vehicle, in which case the traditional 'tip and turn' is quite acceptable.

Volvo rigids began to appear in brewery and soft-drink delivery fleets with the introduction of the FL6-16 model. These were fairly swiftly superseded by the FL617 with the optional turbocharged, six-cylinder, 5.48-litre, 180bhp engine designated the TD61GS. Low – but not ultra-low – deck-heights were the norm for purpose-specified vehicles by the late Eighties, when these two Liverpool-registered vehicles, fitted with air-suspension and low-profile tyres, started life. They are both equipped with Don-Bur Slide-a-Side bodywork which the photograph effectively illustrates in both its travelling and loading modes. Also specified was the optional ZF S6-65 six-speed synchromesh gearbox.

Seen at the time (1986) as being the ultimate in brewery retail distribution vehicles – or drays – this Tetley's 'waggon and drag' certainly incorporates a lot of up-to-date thinking. With the old suspension problems of the Chinese-six now solved, the twin-steer has again become a viable option for multi-drop work. The advantages of twin-steer, as seen in previous chapters, is their ability for axle-loadings to stay legal with a diminishing load. Their disadvantage is usually their restricted lock and consequently large turning circle. As well as the 'waggon', the 'drag', with its centre-axle configuration, also features the ubiquitous Tautliner body. Conventional drawbar trailers, with a wheel at each corner, are notoriously difficult to reverse, but this centre-axle design reverses in much the same way as an artic so is, at least, more predictable! More recent versions of this configuration have enabled the length of the drawbar to be reduced, in some cases to as little as 400 to 500mm, but this requires additional engineering to prevent the two bodies coming into contact when cornering, and also for vertical articulation as experienced, for example, on ramps or hump-backed bridges. The version shown also has a 'load-through' capability, hence the light-alloy portable catwalk between the two components.

The vehicle for pulling pints in the future will undoubtedly be equipped with a host of electronic gadgets to control many aspects of the vehicle's operation. Already fuel, engine and gearbox management systems are commonplace in some of the larger, more highly specified trucks; electronic replacements for the tachograph will eventually be accepted by the legal authorities; devices for switching on lights at dusk, windscreen wipers when it is wet and other luxuries which 100 years of motoring have managed to do without will be offered by the ever-optimistic manufacturers. However, one 'gadget' which could transform the economics of vehicle operation is the in-cab computer. Instead of delivery notes and all the other paperwork which has to accompany a delivery – especially in brewery work, where returned bottles, crates, kegs and pallets have to be accounted for – a simple keypad will be 'loaded' with specific details for each journey. The 'loading' is done from a standard, office computer and gives information to the driver about where his next call is, how to get to it and what to deliver when he's there. The device also has the facility to record, for analysis, the work which is being done so that productivity can be further improved by removing obstacles from the driver's day. The photographs show what the in-cab computer looks like, as well as one of the vehicles – the MAN 22.332 – in which it is fitted.

CHAPTER SEVEN

Where Next?

Forecasting is amongst man's most hazardous pastimes, so it is with trepidation that any predictions are made about the dray, or even the delivery of beer.

Technological forecasting is thwarted not only by ignorance of activities in related fields, other organizations or countries, but by the sheer pace of change, a pace which is itself accelerating and will lead into areas currently beyond imagination. From the beginning of time, man lived in caves for some 650 generations. After 791 generations, printing had been invented, and by 797 generations there was passenger travel at 10mph. The invention of the electric motor and the internal combustion engine arrived a generation later, swiftly followed by passenger travel at 100mph. After 799½ generations computers came onto the scene and within a quarter of a generation of that, not only was passenger travel at 1,000mph a reality but space travel at, say, 18,000mph had also been achieved.

Although the ultimate answer to 'Where Next?' is unforeseeable, there are major factors to influence its direction. One such example is legislation, which in addition to setting out rules for the health, safety and conditions of the workforce, also governs vehicle dimensions. Calls for more axles for a given load, road-friendly suspension and the possible requirement to fit *front* under-run bumpers and so on, are all tending to make the vehicle heavier. Finally, within the last few years changes to the licensing laws have been seen, allowing all-day opening, which introduces new problems and opportunities to the delivery function.

Legislation determines part of another increasingly important contributor to this question: environmental awareness. All vehicle operators now have to take this matter forcibly into consideration as it forms an important part of their application for an operator's licence, which covers areas such as noise and nuisance to neighbours. Operators also have to conform to requirements on exhaust emissions, air-brake silencers, visual intrusion, vibration and much else. Such issues are relevant to customers who, in the enlightened Nineties, are tending to embrace family values to a greater extent. These areas, plus the availability of and attitudes towards fossil fuels, will all affect the future design of the vehicle.

Other influential factors upon productivity concern general trends in goods vehicle design. Many projects, of course, are already on the drawingboard or even in limited production. Examples from the field of general heavy-vehicle technology include the much increased use of plastics in heavy-truck manufacture, and electronics for control of gear-changing and other functions, as well as for engine and fuel management.

At the top end of the range, engines are being made available with the hitherto unheard of power of between 450 and 500bhp. For top-weight vehicles, engine sizes appear to be concentrating around the 11-litre mark, with an alternative set of offerings at around 14 litres. It seems probable that efforts will be directed towards obtaining more power from the same sized engine than towards increasing the engine size itself, but no doubt new, lighter materials will arrive to change this. Some of the latest engine developments include cam-free valve-lifting – controlled electronically through solenoids which can be actuated precisely so as to reduce emissions and improve fuel consumption.

The last few years have also seen the introduction of ABS braking, a trend which is likely to continue, but again electric retarders are already becoming more widespread, so that individual electronic control of braking at each wheel, may yet be seen. Suspension systems may return to being steel-based rather than air-based as the technology improves, and rubber suspensions still remain a serious contender.

Vehicle bodies will be developed with lower centres of gravity and become more aerodynamic, especially once

Originally developed for rapid access to sheet-steel coil on artic trailers, Don-Bur have come up with the *Coverhaul* sliding canopy to allow dray deliveries to be made in restricted access areas. Teamed with a mini-dray, the canopy can easily be worked by a single drayman. It opens either to the front or to the rear and has the advantages that it can be loaded from the top or from the sides. Load retention is by removable aluminium bars on a similar principle to the *boxing-ring* vehicles of the Fifties and Sixties. Perhaps it is true to say that there really is no such thing as a new idea!

A front-wheel-drive chassis/cab by Chassis Developments built for Bass Brewers, photographed before the body was fitted. The objectives with this prototype were to improve ergonomics for one-man operation, to give a low floor height to reduce injuries to draymen and to improve productivity with a 12-tonne payload. Front-wheel drive, and small wheels with air-suspension at the rear, allows a completely flat body-floor height of only 860mm. This Perkins-engined model features ZF automatic transmission, combined with a 'drop' box to position the drive output suitably for the front axle, which has a full 40 degrees of lock. Further to improve manoeuvrability, the rear axle is self-steering, giving a turning circle of only 65ft.

remaining problems of cooling (brakes as well as engines) are overcome. They may also become stiffer or stronger so that, to all intents and purposes, chassis can be dispensed with – a feature which is already making itself felt in semi-trailer design.

With specific regard to developments in the design of the brewer's dray, it appears that Bass, the Burton-on-Trent brewers, have taken the lead in new thinking, as distinct from further developing old thinking. As seen in Chapter 6, Bass have been operating on trial a specially designed dray with a very low deck-height for urban use. To achieve the low deck-height, small-diameter wheels have been used at the rear and, to carry the weight, this has meant duplicating the axles – so the vehicle is a six-wheeler. This introduces two interesting engineering problems to solve.

First, three-axle vehicles are inherently less manoeuvrable than the two-axle variety so, for urban use, three axles become a disadvantage – unless the rear axle itself steers. This is exactly what happens with this prototype, enabling it to 'turn on a sixpence' – or so it seems when driving it!

The second problem is how to transmit the power from the engine, beneath such a low deck, to the front axle of the rear set. This has been overcome by powering the front axle rather than the rear and the engineering to achieve this (carried out by Chassis Developments Ltd) is, indeed, ingenious. The Perkins engine is installed back-to-front so that it drives forwards into a Z-F automatic gearbox mounted above a stepped transfer gearbox which transmits the drive to the front wheels. Add to this the special, easy-access crew cab and improvements to the methods of actually handling the load, and the result is a truly modern urban dray. Time, and operational trials, will dictate whether the idea catches on or is economic, but as a concept vehicle it has much going for it.

Other developments by Bass include a 'walking floor' to assist the drayman with handling containers, coupled with a powered conveyor belt running across the front of the body to assist with the loading of empties.

The impact of Information Technology has and will continue to transform the nature of transport productivity beyond what it is presently possible to envisage. The evolution of the computer means that it is already feasible for electronic management systems to be continually

Another approach to the urban mini-dray, this prototype, from Don-Bur, meets the objective of enhancing one-man dray operation by offering quick access to the sides and rear of the vehicle body, with solid closures rather than curtains for security reasons. The solid side panels open up and angle outwards in a matter of seconds, away from the load, and when fully opened occupy a position above the roof of the vehicle – thus preventing damage to closures when loading by fork-lift truck. Illustrated is the two-door version; a three-door prototype is also available which is capable of operating in an even narrower space. This is lever-operated by means of an eccentric cam located in the front and rear frame. The two top sections lift simultaneously as the bottom section lowers. Each side can be operated independently and locking is by means of a remote hand-held device to which the rear shutter is also connected.

The latest in urban artics supplied to Scottish and Newcastle Beer Production by Marshalls SPV of Cambridge, the long established bodybuilding and general engineering concern which now owns what is left of the old Bedford trucks business. The trailer, grossing 18,000kg, features a special impact-resistant floor, designed to last the life of the trailer. Even with modern handling methods the decks of brewery vehicles suffer hard wear, and *Impadek* flooring, laid transversely, is designed to withstand the shocks of heavy brewery kegs being dropped on it by 'riding' the shock and thus minimizing the damage. Being of aluminium construction it does not adversely affect the tare weight which, for this trailer, is only 3,600kg including the body.

diagnosing an engine for faults and for its findings to be transmitted back to base by satellite. Why should these details not be analyzed by the base computer, which also schedules work through the maintenance workshops, makes a booking for the vehicle and calls it in for service just-in-time, thus increasing the vehicle's overall availability?

Work, the details of which are commercially sensitive, is already in hand in which the vehicle 'system' becomes an extension of the warehouse and administrative systems to enable productivity-enhancing measures to be taken in all three fields of endeavour. It is not beyond reason that other interpretations of the very word 'productivity' may be sought and found. The side of an articulated trailer is the equivalent of an advertising hoarding of a fairly considerable size with, in a typical London-to-Birmingham journey, the number of 'opportunities to see' (an advertising industry measurement) far exceeding that of many television commercials. With a trend towards advertising brands, rather than simply companies, on the sides of vehicles, the drays themselves may yet be considered as highly productive advertising sites which just happen to deliver the product as well!

While being used as advertising media, greater emphasis could also be placed upon the use of the vehicle's livery for safety improvement. Eye-catching and interesting livery is fine so long as the attention of other road-users is not dangerously distracted. Arguments have long raged about lighting and marking large goods vehicles, and new reflective materials can be used to enhance safety. It is already recognized as good practice to paint wheels and 'undercarriage' in lighter colours to make them more visible to cyclists and pedestrians, and no doubt similar ideas and devices will be developed to render the vehicles even safer.

The stage of technological development has almost been reached whereby to dream of something is to see it as reality within a short space of time. In the future, the only forecast that will be made with absolute certainty is that change will be the one constant and, this being the case, the end of productivity development in transport is not yet even in sight.

The shape of things to come. This Mitsubishi urban dray of 10,000kg payload capacity was exhibited at the RAI show in Amsterdam in 1992. Described by the maker as 'the Super Fighter' it embodies many up-to-the-minute features apart from its aerodynamic body shape. Amongst these is a very highly developed floor, manufactured by the British firm, Joloda, consisting of a slat conveyor powered by the truck's electrical system, to assist with handling the load. The mechanism not only minimizes the amount of physical work required from the crew but also reduces the noise made by handling both full and empty containers. This is very much a sign of the times as environmental, and Health and Safety, considerations begin to take precedence in the minds of designers and productivity improvers.

APPENDIX ONE

Weights and Measures

Throughout the text, conversions from metric to Imperial measures have been made except where they would interfere with the general flow of meaning. It seems inappropriate, somehow, to refer to a 6in-wide iron tyre on a 19th century dray as having a dimension of 152.4 millimetres, or even to round it to 150mm, (let alone 15cm!) as these measures were not in use by the manufacturers and craftsmen who would have made them. However, the transport industry is, today, very largely metricated with fuel dispensed in litres, weights denoted in kilograms and dimensions stated in metres. Being British, of course, we cannot state distances in kilometres so we have the anomaly of fuel consumption being stated as miles per litre, whilst the rest of Europe uses 'litres per hundred kilometres'. The European ratio seems far more logical as a measure of consumption as it actually states *consumption* per unit of *distance* whilst 'miles per gallon' measures distance per unit of fuel.

The following tables are much simplified and are only to be used as a guide in interpreting the text where no conversion is given.

Liquid Measure

1 barrel (brl)	=	36 gallons (gall)
1 gallon (gall)	=	8 pints (pt)
1 flagon or quart	=	2 pints
1 litre (ltr)	=	1.760 pints
1 litre	=	0.220 gallons
1 pint	=	0.568 litres
1 gallon	=	4.545 litres

Brewers' Liquid Measure

Cask name	Gallons	Approx. gross weight (kg)
Pin	4	25
Firkin	9	45
Kilderkin	18	90
BARREL	36	180
Hogshead	54	270
Butt	108	540

Avoirdupois and metric equivalents

1 ton	=	20 hundredweights (cwt)
	=	2,240 pounds (lb)
1 hundredweight (cwt)	=	4 quarters (qr)
	=	112lb

1 quarter (qr)	=	2 stones (st)
	=	28lb
1 ton	=	1,018 kilograms (kg)
1 tonne	=	1,000kg
	=	0.982 ton
	=	19cwt 2qr 16lb

Linear Measure

1 metre	=	1.094 yards (yd)
	=	3 feet (ft) 3.37 inches (in)
	=	39.37in
1 yard	=	0.9144 metres (m)
	=	91.44 centimetres (cm)
	=	914.4 millimetres (mm)
1 foot	=	304.8mm
1 inch	=	25.4mm

Some handy approximations are:

25mm	=	1in
100mm	=	4in
300mm	=	1ft

APPENDIX TWO

Where Are They Now?

This appendix contains a list, arranged in alphabetical order, of all the vehicle manufacturers mentioned, either in the text or in the picture captions, in this book. For readers who require a greater level of detail – this list gives only the very briefest of mentions – there are many books referring to single makes and, for a brief history of each individual make, regardless of country of origin, there are also several reference works. Appendix Three lists a short, selected bibliography.

AEC
Southall
1912–1968. Originally The Associated Equipment Co, at Walthamstow, London, up to 1926. Acquired by Leyland in 1968.

Albion
Glasgow
1902–1972. Acquired by Leyland in 1951.

Allchin
Northampton
1905–1931.

Armstrong-Saurer
Newcastle-on-Tyne
1931–1937. Built under licence from Saurer of Switzerland; the licence passed to Morris Commercial cars in 1937.

Atkinson
Preston
1910–1975. Acquired by Seddon in 1970 and taken over by International Harvester in 1974. Later passed to Enasa (20% owned by Daimler Benz; 60% by MAN and 20% by the Spanish State) and ultimately under MAN ownership.

Austin
Birmingham
1908–1970. BMC 1961–1967; BLMC 1970–1977; see Leyland.

Aveling & Porter
Rochester
1865–1932. Acquired by AGE combine in 1919 who allocated their production to Richard Garrett & Sons.

AWD
Luton
(All-Wheel Drive) acquired Bedford Truck and Bus from General Motors Corporation (USA) in November 1987. Into receivership 1992.

Bayley
North London
1899–1901. Predecessor of the Straker company.

Bedford
Luton
1931–1987. Originally 'GMC's British commercial', went into liquidation in 1987; acquired by AWD Ltd; into receivership 1992; acquired by Marshalls of Cambridge (who supplied Bedford bodies during the war).

Belsize
Manchester
1906–1925.

Beyer Peacock
Manchester
1903–1914. Also known as the Gorton.

Bretherton & Bryan
Colchester
1905–1908. Vendors of Davey Paxman traction engines. In 1906 changed their name to Bryan & Co.

Burrell
Thetford
1856–1932. Joined Avelings and Garretts as part of the AGE combine in 1919.

Carter
Rochdale
1906 to date. Company still exists but waggon building ceased in 1909.

Chevrolet
Detroit, Michigan, USA
1918 to date. Division of General Motors and predecessor of Bedford in the UK.

Clayton
Lincoln
1918–1930. Formerly Clayton & Shuttleworth, 1894–1926.

Commer
London until 1906, then Luton 1905–1976. Acquired by Humber in 1926; Rootes Group 1933; Chrysler UK 1973; now part of RVI.

Coulthard
Preston
1895–1907. Taken over by Leyland in 1907.

DAF
Eindhoven, Netherlands
1938 to date. Merged with British Leyland UK in April 1987.

Daimler
Stuttgart, Germany
1896–1926.
Coventry
1897–1972. Thence British Leyland qv.

Dennis
Guildford
1904 to date. Acquired by Hestair 1978. Later formed part of Trinity Holdings.

Deutz
Cologne, Germany
1926–1936. Acquired by Magirus in 1938; now part of Iveco.

English
Hebden Bridge
1903–1907.

ERF
Sandbach
1933 to date. Rival firm to Foden, set up by E R Foden.

Foden
Sandbach
1887 to date. In 1980 became a wholly-owned subsidiary of Paccar (USA – builders of Kenworth and Peterbilt trucks). Renamed Sandbach Engineering Co.

Ford
Manchester to 1931, Dagenham from 1931 1911 to date. Plants added at Langley, Bucks in 1960 and Southampton in 1971.

Foster
Lincoln
1904–1934.

Fowler
Leeds
1880–1935.

Garrett
Leiston
1856–1960. Acquired Caledon Motor Co in 1926, but in 1932 collapsed along with the rest of the AGE (Agricultural and General Engineers) combine. Thereafter concentrated on electric vehicles and eventually ceased production of commercials.

Guy
Wolverhampton
1914–1968. Acquired by Jaguar Cars and became part of British Leyland in 1968.

Halley
Glasgow
1901–1935. Bought by Albion Motors.

Hallford
Dartford
1907–1925.

Harrods
Knightsbridge, London
1937–1939.

Hercules
Manchester
1903–1909. Firms by the name of Hercules have also existed in Switzerland, Germany and the USA.

Hindley
Bourton
1904–1908.

Iveco
France, Italy, Germany, UK
1974 to date. Amalgamation of FIAT, OM and Magirus Deutz; now incorporates the Ford Truck business in the UK.

Jesse Ellis
Maidstone
1899–1907. Sometimes known simply as Ellis.

Karrier
Huddersfield, Luton and Dunstable under various different owners
1908 to date. Originally Clayton & Co (at Huddersfield); renamed Karrier 1920; moved to Luton 1934; acquired by Rootes Group 1968; acquired by Chrysler UK 1970; now part of RVI – Renault Vehicles Industriel.

Latil	Suresnes, France 1898–1956. Merged with Renault and Somua in 1955 to form Saviem.
Leyland	Leyland 1896 to date. Originally Lancashire Steam Motor Co; renamed Leyland Motors 1907; Leyland Motor Corporation 1963; BLMC (British Leyland Motor Corporation) Truck & Bus Division 1968; Leyland Vehicles 1978; Leyland DAF since April 1987.
Lifu	(Liquid Fuel Engineering Co) East Cowes, Isle of Wight 1897–1905.
Londonderry	Durham 1903–1908.
MAN	Nurnberg, Germany 1915 to date. Builders of the first diesel engine (1897). Commercial vehicle production from 1915.
Mann	Leeds 1897–1928. Originally Mann & Charlesworth to 1900; receivership 1926; liquidation 1928.
Maudslay	Coventry 1903–1942; Alcester 1943–1960. Gradual merger with AEC, complete by 1954; name discontinued 1960.
Mercedes-Benz	Stuttgart, Germany and many other locations, worldwide. 1926 to date.
Morris Commercial	Cowley 1914–1970; Austin-Morris Division BLMC 1970–1977; see Leyland.
Napier	Lambeth, London 1901–1920. From 1920 concentrated on aero-engines.
Orwell	Ipswich 1915–1928. Model name for electric vehicles built by Ransomes, Sims & Jefferies (qv).
Pagefield	Wigan 1907–1955. Parent company (Walker Bros Engineering) acquired in 1947 by another, untraced, engineering company.

Ransomes Ransomes, Sims and Jefferies	Ipswich 1842–1946. An offshoot still produces off-road electrics for special purposes.
Renault	Billancourt, France 1900 to date; see RVI.
Robertson	Fleetwood 1903–1912.
Robey	Lincoln 1862–1934.
RVI	(Renault Vehicles Industriel), Billancourt, France 1900 to date. In 1956 merged with Floirat, Latil and Somua to become Societe Anonyme de Vehicules Industriels et Equipments Mecaniques (SAVIEM); acquired Berliet in 1974, American Motors and Mack (USA) in 1978; in 1981 acquired control of Peugeot-Citroen's Dodge factories in Britain and Spain.
Saurer	Arbon, Switzerland 1903 to date. Acquired Berna in 1929; now part of the Mercedes-Benz empire.
Scammell	Spitalfields, London to 1921, then Watford 1919 to date under Unipower ownership. Acquired by Leyland in 1955, later merged production with Thornycroft and ultimately sold the 'heavy' end of the business to Unipower.
Scania	Malmo, Sweden, 1903–1911; Scania-Vabis 1911–1969; Saab-Scania, Sodertalje, 1969 to date.
Seddon	Oldham 1938–1975. Acquired by International Harvester in 1974 and merged with Atkinson in 1975. See Atkinson for Seddon's subsequent history.
Sentinel	Shrewsbury 1906–1956. Originally Alley & McClellan, Polmadie, Glasgow to 1917; factory acquired by Rolls-Royce in 1956 and production discontinued.
Somua	Saint-Ouen, France 1914–1955. See RVI
SM	London 1904–1912. Production of commercials took place in 1910 only.

Stewart	Glasgow 1902–1910. Licensed by Thornycroft.	Volvo	Gothenberg, Sweden 1928 to date.
St Pancras	Holloway, London 1903–1911. In 1911 manufacturing rights were passed to the SM company.	Vulcan	Southport 1907–1938; 1938 acquired by Tilling Stevens and moved to Maidstone, Kent; 1953 acquired by Rootes Group.
Straker	Bristol 1899–1912. At different times known as Bayley-Straker and Straker-Squire.	Walker	Wigan 1947–1955.
Tasker	Andover 1902–1925. Ultimately became part of Craven Industries, producing Craven Tasker trailers.	Wallis & Steevens	Basingstoke 1895–1930.
Thames	Greenwich, London 1905–1913. All marketing activity taken over by Motor Coaches Ltd in 1911.	Wantage	Wantage 1901–1913.
Thornycroft	Chiswick, London (initially) 1896–1977. Absorbed into the Leyland empire and ceased production as part of Scammell Motors.	Yorkshire	Leeds 1903–1938. A branch of the Deighton's Flue & Tube Co and not separately incorporated during the period of commercial vehicle production.

APPENDIX THREE

Selected Bibliography

The following is a brief list of sources and suggestions for further reading. It is by no means an exhaustive or comprehensive list, being a selection of some of the sources referred to in preparing this book. The topic of commercial road transport is still growing in popularity and for those whose appetite has been whetted by this volume it is suggested that they join the mailing list of one of the specialist transport publishers. Regrettably, some of the books mentioned are now out of print.

Transport History – General

Commercial Motor Road Transport
L M Meyrick-Jones   Pitman

Early Days on the Road (1819–1941)
Lord Montagu & G N Georgano   Michael Joseph

Economic Survey of British Transport from the 17th to the 20th Century
Dyos & Aldcroft   Pelican

One Hundred Years of Motoring
Flower & Wynn Jones   RAC

The Long Haul
M Seth-Smith   Hutchinson Benham

Traffic & Transport
G L Turnbull   G Allen & Unwin

Transport Revolution 1750–1850
P J G Ransom   World's Work

Transport Saga   Privately published by Hay's Wharf

Reference Books

Complete Encyclopaedia of Commercial Vehicles
Georgano & Marshall Naul   Motorbooks International

Illustrated Encyclopaedia of Trucks & Buses
D Miller   Hamlyn

The World's Commercial Vehicles
G N Georgano   Temple Press

General

Horse-Drawn Vehicles
A Ingram   Blandford

Steam on the Road
D Gladwin   Batsford

'Single Make' Titles

ERF; Scania; Seddon Atkinson; MAN; DAF; Dennis; Volvo; Scammell; FIAT; AEC; International; Berliet; Magirus; Leyland (World Trucks Series)
P Kennett   Patrick Stephens

DAF; Scania; Mercedes-Benz (Trucks Today Series)
E Gibbins   MRP

Bedford – GM's British Commercial
M Sedgwick   Beaulieu Books

Ford – The Big Idea
(Compiled by D Hacket)   Ford

Scammell Vehicles
(Compiled by B Vanderveen)   Nynehead Books

Originally a coal cart and converted for brewery use, this dray was used as a hearse at the funeral of one of the Young family in 1990 – the ultimate demonstration of transport's versatility!